ENJO
THE
JOURNEY!

9/12/19

D1290409

ENJOY
THE
JOURNEY!

3/6/19

The Inspirational Blueprint for Helping Young
Professionals *with* Career-Centric Life Skills

LEVEL-UP

TO PROFESSIONAL

Elevate Your Success at
Business, Work & Life

Scott Abbott

Background Information & Some Legal Mumbo Jumbo

In 2007, Scott Abbott wrote an "edu-taining" guidance book called Pocket PorchLights. Scott's mission for writing the book was to help young adults - and by extension schools, teachers, families, communities and employers - with career-centric life skills. Since being published, Pocket PorchLights has won lots of praise, and many accolades. It's been used within education and organizations across the planet; earned an award from Disney, and has become a statistical best-seller. In addition to the book itself, Scott has also done over 100 motivational talks, speeches and guest lectures to 10,000+ students, teachers, faculty and parents – at high schools, colleges, companies and functions. Suffice it to say, the book has done great, and to this day makes a very positive impact on many lives. Now, fast forward to 2014. As you can see from the book in your hands (or device, as the case may be) - Scott has written and produced a truly inspiring, "leveled-up" sequel edition to Pocket PorchLights. Level-UP to Professional has all of the best-of-the-best content (and messaging) from Pocket PorchLights, but also includes new, refreshed, and updated copy, an innovative and vibrant copy design and layout, a new chapter on Personal Branding, and a new Afterword section with fun and important questions for both individual and group discussions/exercises. So, while Pocket PorchLights served us well from 2007 through 2013 ... Level-UP to Professional is here to serve us from 2014, and beyond. Enjoy the book.

Copyright © 2014 by Scott Abbott & Level-UP, Corp.

All rights reserved. No part of this publication may be reproduced, distributed or transmitted in any form or means, including photocopying, recording, or other electronic or mechanical methods, without the prior written permission of the author and publisher, except in the case of brief quotations embodied in reviews and certain other noncommercial uses permitted by copyright law.

For rights permission, media, speaking and/or advisory requests, contact:

kathy@leveluptopro.com

To purchase volume book orders (25+), visit www.leveluptopro.com.

And join us on Facebook at www.facebook.com/leveluptopro.

Level-UP to Professional / Scott Abbott. —1st edition.

ISBN-13: 978-0615929293

ISBN-10: 061592929X

This book is dedicated to

My Family

It's also dedicated to

You and Your Family

Family is Good

BUT business is business! And business must grow…

regardless of crummies in tummies, you know.

UNLESS someone like you cares a whole awful lot,

nothing is going to get better. It's not.

Dr. Seuss
The Lorax

CONTENTS

INTRODUCTION

My Purpose and Gratitude

{**WARNING:** <u>Don't</u>. <u>You</u>. <u>Dare</u>. <u>Skip</u>. <u>This</u>. <u>Section</u>. Yeah, I know… lots of people blow right on by the introduction in books, because they don't think it's all that important, and maybe because they're just plain lazy (psst: I do it myself, so don't sweat it). But trust me — you have to read this introduction: it sets up the whole book. In fact, I really think it's make or break, do or die (well, maybe not that harsh). Besides, you don't want to be getting into trouble this early in our relationship; I know where to find you, and there will be retribution. Oh, and be sure to turn on your happy face while reading. And do it now. Otherwise, as *they* say, the beatings will continue until morale improves. And who knows, there might be something in it about finding a hidden treasure. Just saying. So if you don't want to crash and burn in business, work and life (aw snap, I did it again… I got on your case, even before you deserved it), than please read the intro okay, for all our sakes. Cool?}

"Take away the cause, and the effect ceases."

MIGUEL DE CERVANTES

Greetings and Salutations

On behalf of the many people who helped me develop this book, I hope that you and those you love are happy, and doing great. If by chance you're graduating from school, starting a new job, or just trying a new approach to work and/or life — then congratulations, and best of luck.

Carpe Diem, Yo.

While I'm handing out the kudos, I'd also like to thank all of the people who inspire me, for that matter. Thanks to their guidance, support and friendship... in addition to the influence from hundreds of others... I feel pretty confident that the following pages (moreover, the real-world, been-there/done-that insights, observations, and recommendations)... will complement your classroom knowledge, as well as your previous experiences... and be an asset to your current and future endeavors.

Does that sound good?

Last, but certainly not least, I want to thank you — **yeah you!** —— for grabbing this book, and being a DOER. Even better, for being someone who <u>gets things done</u>. Sure, I know you've got a bunch of stuff going on, and a boatload of other things that you could be doing (the list is long, right?). But still, you made the time to check this out, and give it a go. Indeed, you took the initiative to read something new that just might help you achieve more success in business, work and life.

For that, I applaud you.

(CLAP, CLAP, CLAP, CLAP, CLAP, CLAP)

However.

If it is not your **destination, aspiration** or **motivation** to improve yourself **personally** and **professionally**, then feel free to drop this book like a bad habit (unless of course it's for a class grade, than you better hang in there), and get back to the other stuff you've got to get done.

I won't take it personally, for the most part.

On the other hand — if you're cool with this agenda, i.e. to help you improve your **career-centric life skills**, then cue the soundtrack, and...

Let's get this party started.

By way of background, you've inevitably heard of the "level-up" expression as used in video gaming, right? Personally, I'm kinda partial to the classic, old-school gems like *Donkey Kong, Space Invaders, Galaga, Tetris* and *Frogger*; although I do enjoy some new-school games that let me dance, battle and hangout with family and friends.

(We interrupt this programming, to suggest that if for some reason, you have not heard of the "level-up" expression (this applies to you too, gramps) — well then, props to you for figuring out how to get to where you are... while living under your rock, on your own personal planet. Yes, I went there. Now, back to our regularly scheduled broadcast.)

If you think about it from a deeper perspective, the term "level-up" actually recognizes ambition, inspiration and achievement; celebrating past accomplishments, current capabilities and future possibilities.

(And you thought it was just about gaming.)

But level-up is more than just a term.
Much more.

Level-up is an action-oriented hybridization of a:

mandate

campaign

mantra

mission

philosophy

(you get the picture)

… to energize life's work, and take you to the next level**S** of success:

Today | Tomorrow | Forever

Now, since you're the kind of person who believes in having a level-up "manifesto" and therefore evidently likes to improve yourself (you do, don't you?) — I'm also going to assume that you already have some of the attributes that are essential to success in business, work and life.

Attributes like…

COMPASSION

ACCOUNTABILITY

DETERMINATION

INITIATIVE

COURAGE

... and the multi-tasking wherewithal to juggle work, play, and relationships. Great stuff. Even better, by the time you're done with this book, I sincerely hope that you'll be even more equipped, to help you deal with the realities *and* surrealities that arise in everyday situations.

More Equipped is Good.

Charlton Ogburn Jr., a prolific author of a dozen books, wrote, *"being unready and ill-equipped is what you have to expect in life."* He calls it our *"universal predicament."* Granted, we often go unprepared into our adventures, and it's a given that we can't know what we don't know.

Be that as it may, we should always do our very best to be honest and forthright about what we actually do know... as opposed to what we think we can figure out once we get there. After all, being new and unprepared is difficult enough as it is, especially if we can help it.

But being busted as a rotten, stinking phony is worse.

Rotten, Stinking Phonies are Bad.

In any event, that's really what this book's purpose, is all about:

1. Getting you better prepared and more confident.

2. Helping you avoid a few missteps (not all, but some).

3. Becoming a better person, and a better professional.

4. And ultimately, being happy and more successful.

Those are the goals.

Goals are Good.

So, what do you think?

Is a book like this worth the price of admission? Which in this case I guess, is the cost of the book, and the time spent reading it. More importantly however, the **value** of the book are the upsides and benefits of learning new things, having a little fun in the process and hopefully, after it's all read and done, being a better/smarter/happier person for it.

> Not too shabby of a deal, if I do say so myself.

If this book happened to make it into one of those MasterCard TV commercials (can you say daydreamer), it might go something like this:

-   Price of the book: around $15 bucks.

-   Time spent writing it: over ten years.

-   Time spent reading it: about three hours.

-   Upside benefit of learning new stuff, and getting absolutely motivated to live a better, happier, more successful work-life…

Priceless.

So, that's what you get out of the book.

What do I get out of it?

Well, in the spirit of total disclosure, I've written this for you and your family, because I consider it my heartfelt civic-duty to help. But I also did it for myself (darn that ego), my kids (who think it would be pretty cool for their dad to write a book), and for my family and friends, who suggest I should put my thoughts and recommendations into written words (I think that really means, that they're tired of hearing me talk).

Encouragement is Good.

In any event, it's not about me.

It's about you, and helping you be the best that you can be.

While we're on the full disclosure track, it's important to declare that what's written in these pages stems from my past experiences, as well as my interpretations of many things. Who we are, what we think, and how we behave, are byproducts of all that we do, see and experience. In other words, we get influenced by almost everything. The trick is in deciding which things to come into contact with, and how much to let those things influence who we are, what we do, and how we behave.

Understand?

That said, I don't always remember who deserves credit, or everyone I should thank (or reprimand), for what I have to say. What's funny is, I've got a really great memory: it's just too darn short (get it?!). This could have something to do with what my wife thinks (and rightfully so), is a case of adult ADD. But I do love her, and my kids... and my parents and my brothers and sister... and their families... and my in-laws... and my dogs who are always happy to see me... and I also like ice cream, blueberry pie, lasagna, sushi, barbecue... hmmm, I wonder what's for dinner? Oh yea, so the fact that I have suspect recollection, and a wavering attention span — requires me to thank everybody I've known, and everything I've seen and read, for the help and inspiration.

Finally, I want to thank you for your commitment to being better:

MENTALLY

EMOTIONALLY

PHYSICALLY

SPIRITUALLY

Better is Good.

I wish you all the best for a great career, and a fantastic life.

And I really hope that you enjoy the book.

Furthermore, I hope that it helps you **Level-UP to Professional**.

@ Business, Work & Life

Because you my friend… you yourself… are the **architect**, **builder** and **custodian** of your own success. It's your house. And while this book can be a "blueprint" to help you get on the right track, you alone are the one responsible for making what you want, come true. You know that.

So good luck.

Even better, make your own luck.

> **LUCK**, after all, is what happens when **PREPERATION** meets **OPPORTUNITY**.

> Don't ever forget that.

BE GOOD.

Scott

PS.1

As you will see throughout the book (and once again, I'm putting my unwavering faith in you, that you are actually reading this introduction, right?)... I frequently use and make references to movies, songs, books, quotes, metaphors, analogies, words and sayings... that given your age and experiences... you may not have heard of, or understand. Up to now. For the record, that's intentional and mostly done for two reasons. 1) Because I just like to (it's kind of *my thing*), and think that they fit the vibe and occasion, so to speak. 2) Because I also think that many of these are "classics" and as such, something that you should know about sooner, not later (that very sentiment being a major point of this book, after all). Be that as it may, let me suggest that if you don't know something that I write or reference... and if it doesn't make sense to you in the meaning and/or context of its use in the book... than take it offline, and check it out for yourself, online. Much more better than using the Internet, go ask your parents, grandparents, teachers, aunts, uncles, baristas (strike that) to help with your comprehension. After all, that do-it-yourself extracurricular homework is part of the leveling-up journey. When in doubt, figure it out: on your own, and/or partner-up.

PS.2

I'm going to assume that you like good music. After all, life and music go together, just like warm cookies and cold milk. That said, this book is influenced by songs and their lyrics. Music also motivated me while writing (and re-writing) this book. So, to enhance your overall reading experience, I encourage you to listen to good music while you read.

And keep listening to good music.

Now and forever.

Good Music is Good.

LEVEL-UP

TO PROFESSIONAL

Elevate Your Success at
Business, Work & Life

ADMISSIONS AND APPRECIATIONS

Why We Do, What We Do

"Knowing is not enough, we must apply.
Willing is not enough, we must do."

JOHAN VON GOETHE

We've all heard people say:

"If I only knew *then,*
what I know *now.*"

Well, the problem with this kind of silly, nonsensical, wont-ever-happen, wishful yearning… is that it's all about the past, not the future.

And we can't change the past.

Nope.

But what if we rearrange that concept to an achievable reality, like:

"If I only knew *now,*
what I'll know *then.*"

The phrase becomes useful, not useless.

Now, it's meaningful and relevant.

That's because we're leveraging other people's <u>hindsight</u>, passed on to us as <u>insight</u>. By extension, we get to use that <u>insight,</u> as our own <u>foresight</u>.

Foresight is Good.

Henry Ford said, that before everything else,

"Getting ready and being prepared,
is the secret to success."

And that's what this book is all about:

✓ **Helping you get fit and ready,**

✓ **Staying fit and ready, and**

✓ **Accelerating your success.**

Now admittedly, I was one of those new young employees, that didn't prepare properly; I learned a lot of stuff the harder way. You see, while I graduated from college with decent grades and lots of "I know better" assumptions, I was still highly unprepared, and to my detriment, overconfident, nonetheless. Guilty as charged. Especially in terms of what I *thought* I *knew* about business and people, and how my life, inside and outside of work, was going to change me, as well as those around me. Heck, I could write a book about what I didn't know about business, work and life (he types with a wink ;). Even worse, what I lacked in readiness and preparation… I made up for in false bravado. It was not a good strategy, and I was ultimately forced to (gulp) change.

Change is difficult.
Even good change.

While there may be something to learning "on the job," through the "school of hard knocks," or even "baptism by fire," it doesn't mean that we shouldn't look for help, do our homework, and be prepared.

After all, a nice pat-on-the-back for a job well-done… is a heck of a lot better than the proverbial hard kick-in-the-butt, for a job done-poorly.

Reprimands are Bad.
(but sometimes helpful)

One of the biggest mistakes that we can make is assuming that we'll get off to a great start with our new jobs; become invaluable employees from the very first day; enjoy loads of fun and lots of happiness, and be largely rewarded for our work through lots of props, and bankable coin.

Guess what?

It's probably not going to happen. Even if we're gutsy, book-smart, talented or school-trained to do specific jobs. In fact, it's dangerous to overestimate ourselves, thinking that we can just show up and hit-the-ground-running. Frankly, it doesn't matter if you're the new intern, or the new mayor: regardless of the job, you're not going to completely know what you need to do... or what it's all about... until you do it.

And then do it some more.

Even common sense (or Spidey senses),
won't help us out completely.

Because the fact is,

Common Sense Is Not So Common.

(And you're not Spider-Man.)

As Mark Twain said,

> *"It ain't what you don't know that gets you into trouble.*
> *It's what you know that just ain't so."*

How true.

Or take singer/songwriter John Mayer, who sings so eloquently about the bittersweet "train of life." No, we can't stop it. And sure, the ride will be bumpy and discouraging sometimes, and we'll have to travel with some unlikable passengers. But there will be more times when the ride is smooth and encouraging, with lots of likeable companions, especially if we have the right attitude and the right support.

This means that you can't just wait around for the world to change in your favor. (Sorry to disagree with you on that one, Mr. Mayer.)

Waiting on the world to change, is not realistic, and not all that smart.

The fact is, your time is here, and you're time is now (with a nod to another J.M. — John Mellencamp). You're the future and the present, so get onboard and be a good passenger. Better yet, jump-in the front seat, buckle-up and help drive. After all, nobody likes a backseat driver.

Nobody.

Speaking of your likeable companions (he writes humbly) — this is probably a good time to give you some more info about myself. After all, it might help to get to know me a little better, so you can feel more comfortable with me, and more confident about what I have to say.

Mostly, I think it's important to admit what I know, and what I don't (which is an awful lot) — and why I'm compelled to write this book.

So here goes:

For starters, let's just say that I've had a number of significant experiences in my life so far: great ones, good ones, bad ones and sad ones… and that's all within my first forty-something years. Like everyone else in this world, I also have much more to learn, and a lot of growing up to do (parents call that "maturing" — whatever).

But that's all right, because the day we think we know it all, or stop having fun and lose our desire to improve and be much more better…

physically

mentally

emotionally

spiritually

… well, that day shouldn't happen, because people are never "*done*."

And we don't just improve for our own sake, but on the behalf of all the people who love us, depend on us, or just have to deal with us.

You see, life's more than a two-way street: it's a multi-lane highway, with lots of roundabouts and stop lights.

And make no mistake: improving ourselves isn't always easy.

It's not.

But what carries us through this constant state of self-improvement, is the recognition that improving ourselves isn't just about us as individuals; it's also about those who love us, need us, and depend on us. Vise-versa, it's about those that we love, need, and depend on. Think of that as our,

"Personal Ecosystem"

From a business perspective, I've had both failure, and success. I've launched several technology companies, and one very hip restaurant. In addition to starting new companies, I've also acquired, managed and sold some, as well. Complementing my direct, hands-on leadership experience, I've advised hundreds of organizations, big and small.

But before all of those corporate gigs — during junior high, high school and college — I worked as a busboy, dishwasher, bartender, caddy, waiter, house-painter, janitor, and cook. I also interned, and did paid stints in retail, a newsroom, radio station, warehouse and theatre.

Working and Employment are Good. (especially the paychecks generated)

Taken together, between my early days and later, I've had lots of jobs, and worked with lots of different companies: from small, agile, boot-strapped, super-cool, play-foosball-in-the-office, hi-tech start-ups... to massive, inflexible, not-so-cool, don't-play-foosball-in-the-office, low-tech conglomerates. And throughout it all, I've been inspired by leaders and tolerated fools; learning commendable attributes from admirable people, and suffering intolerable behavior from unbearable jerks.

Jerks suck.
Big time.

Now, from a personal perspective, I'm fortunate to have love in my life, as well as happiness and good health. But in years past, I've been miserable and dejected, just like most people, some of the time. I've been worth worthless millions (on paper, as they say), and been totally flat broke. There was even a time when I was depressingly alone and afraid, painfully unemployed and sold most of my stuff just to eat.

Bummed and broke isn't the funnest thing in the world. I know.

Thankfully, after all of that living, I am now a relatively secure and reasonably adjusted man (so says me). I'm blessed to live in a nice town, and in a loving home; with a remarkable wife, two great kids, insatiable dogs, and a lazy frog that I swear will outlive us all. (Heck, it's starting to sound like a Mellencamp song, albeit a boring one.)

Truly, life's a blessing: bumps, scrapes, bruises and all.

Life is Good.

To recap: I've seen some, done some, won some, lost some.
I've experienced the highs and lows of victory and defeat.

That said, I don't claim to know everything or be perfect in any way — faaarrr from it. Like everyone, I have much more to see, do, learn, love, and improve upon (trust me). And with hard work and God's good grace, I hope to be given the don't-ever-take-it-for-granted opportunity to do so.

Now then, while I can't claim to be an expert in all facets of people, business, work and life — I have seen enough good and bad behavior in all four, to have opinions about what works, and what doesn't.

Moreover, I'm constantly amazed, baffled and bewildered by how many businesspeople — supposedly even well-educated, experienced and successful ones — don't seem to get some of the basic and appropriate **qualities**, **attributes** and **appreciations** that it takes to be *good* businesspeople, with a specific emphasis on the "good people" part. (That's not the rule, mind you, but sadly, it's not uncommon.)

That's why the world needs you and your peers to be good.

Because you are the next generation of leaders.
Eventually and inevitably, you and your generation
will be in charge of our businesses, government,
environment and the entire planet.

No pressure.

Above and beyond being the boss and ruling the universe… you're also someone's child, grandchild and eventually if you so choose (if you're not already), you might even be someone's parent. That's when you'll understand my motivation, and that of other parents. It's true.

You see, most parents want their children to be safe and happy — ready, willing and able to handle all that life has to dish out. And life as we know it, is truly a magnificent, glorious and bountiful feast... even though it's often messy, and at times, can require lots of napkins (and maybe even some hefty paper towels, for those extra sloppy moments).

Now unfortunately, while most parents want what's best for their kids, they may not always say it, show it, or act like it. One of the problems is that some parents over-praise and over-pacify (aka "spoil"), which on the surface might not seem like a big deal... but over time, can set the kids up for a tougher transition, when they go to make it on their own.

Can you say problem?

This type of coddling can lead to the "Stuart Smalley" factor. (FYI: Stuart Smalley was a goofy character played by Senator Al Franken, back in his *Saturday Night Live* days). In the skit, Smalley used the self-affirmation, "Because I'm good enough, I'm smart enough, and doggonit, people like me." But in reality, it wasn't true. He wasn't good enough, he wasn't smart enough, and no, most people didn't like him.

And why?

Because he needed coddling. And my bet is, his parents had something to do with his situation. (Yeah I know, it was just a funny SNL skit, but what the heck, I'm using it anyway to make an example. I think.)

Worse than coddling and good intentions gone awry, some bad parents condone, propagate and administer the disappointing attitude that the heavy metal band Korn (yeah, I had my long-hair, head-banger days) rallied against in one of its songs when they wondered, and justifiably so, why a parent would ever make their own child feel like a "nobody."

Regretably, that does happen too.
And that's a big-time shame.

The biggest big-time shame, however, is that there are some nefarious parents and predatory adults, who are abusive and downright criminal in their treatment of children. As shocking as those sins are to think about or comprehend, it does unfortunately happen. All we can hope is that the children who are physically and emotionally abused can get out of that situation to find peace and happiness. Personally, I believe the abused get extra credit in heaven. Conversely, I believe the inexcusable deviants that do the abusing, get appropriately and disproportionately punished on this earth, and after they leave it. Good riddance.

Thankfully however, abusive parents and reprehensible adults, are in the extreme minority. They really are. The majority of us... even the absent, neglectful and incarcerated... love and appreciate our children.

It's in our DNA.

And you can't change DNA.

But as parents, we know that we won't always be there to guide and protect you, especially now, as a working adult. That's why you need to do what you need to do; be your own person; make your own way.

In fact, that's a lot of what being a responsible, personally accountable professional adult is all about... assuming you choose to be one.

You do, don't you?

(sure you do)

IT'S OVER, AND
IT'S JUST BEGUN

Keeping Momentum, While Driving Progress

"It's never too late to be who you might have been."

GEORGE ELIOT

In 2001, I was asked to be the Entrepreneur in Residence at Indiana University. What an honor! The job was easy enough, as all I really had to do was spend a couple of carefree days on IU's Bloomington campus, visit with their faculty, students and parents, and talk with them about business, work and life: three of my favorite subjects.

Suffice it to say, I had a great time, and it's still a terrific memory.

As an added bonus, it sparked the aha-moment! to write this book.

Inspiration is Good.

Now, due to my own circumstances at the time, and that the graduating students were dealing with their own set of issues and uncertainty specific to work and life after college, I focused my presentations and conversations on three topics that impacted all of us and our situation:

Reality

Change

Attitude

I figured that was not an easy time for any of us in regard to those aspects. Indeed, it was a time of uncertainty, for all of us. But to paraphrase U2's song, "Zooropa," <u>uncertainty can be a guiding light</u>.

That's a pretty cool perspective, don't you think?

Now, before arriving on campus, I prepared a PowerPoint presentation titled, **"It's Over, and It's Just Begun."** By using this title and framework, I hoped to parallel my world with that of the students, and also to reflect on how this outlook was applicable to life in general.

While the title, at first impression, might seem somewhat glum and pessimistic, depending on your disposition of choice (like whether the clichéd cup is half-full or half-empty (hint: <u>the right answer is **BOTH**</u>), the content, emphasis and message were absolutely the opposite.

The objectives of my talks were to inspire and motivate sensibly. But I also wanted to be candid, real-world and conversational. Although I was a guest speaker and was tasked to give "lectures," I didn't want to lecture. After all, nobody likes lectures, *per se*. We like conversations; being spoken with, not spoken to. And those aren't just semantics.

There's a difference.

With that in mind, I wanted to engage with the students and have meaningful dialogue that respected their intelligence and potential. After all, I've always been a big fan and advocate of a great quote from the author and playwright, Johann von Goethe, in which he wrote,

"Treat people as if they were what they ought to be, and you help them to become what they are capable of being."

Happily, our conversations went extremely well. Booya!

I was humbled by how many students liked what we had to talk about; that they commented favorably on the message, and felt that my words were applicable to them as they were preparing for their own transitions.

And although I was only on campus for a few days, the experience was an inspiration at that juncture in my life, and throughout my life since.

Motivation is Good.

Since having those conversations with the students, the phrase "it's over, and it's just begun" has become both a creed and a mantra in my life. In fact (and you could put this one under the category of too-much-information), I might even have that phrase and/or it's "sentimentality" tattooed on my body, if I wasn't afraid of needles and a reprimand from my parents. (Yeah, the thought of a parent's scorn/rebuke/reprimand can affect you, even when you're 40-something. Trust me.)

When you think about it, "it's over, and it's just begun" — isn't just some lame, bumper-sticker, sound-bite, all-encompassing catch-phrase for one-time events like graduating from school, getting a new job, or having to start working for a living, although those certainly do apply.

The fact is, almost everything that we have to do and/or deal with has a beginning, and an end. No duh, right? But really, most everything's cyclical: School starts, school ends. Jobs start, jobs end. Companies start, they end. Relationships start, and they can end. Most profoundly of all, life begins and life ends, at least the physical form as we know it.

As the ubiquitous, over-used, all-encompassing sound-bite goes:

"it is what it is"

But wait.

Before you think I'm being fatalistic or cavalier, please know that I really do appreciate that some beginnings, and endings, are much more difficult than others, requiring special mindfulness and comprehension.

The more we value that things begin and end — the more we need to enjoy the here and now. If we can successfully harness what we learn through life's beginnings, endings and in-betweens — the better we can navigate and manage the new beginnings, endings and in-betweens.

Does that make sense?

By the way, <u>fate</u> and <u>destiny</u> have nothing to do with anything. They're an absurd excuse disguised as bogus rational. After all, Darth Vader was wrong: it wasn't Luke's destiny to go to the dark side. Was it?

Our destiny is what we make of it. As George Eliot said,

> ## *"It's never too late,*
> ## *to be who you might have been."*

(think about it)

Unless we just want to give up and disappoint ourselves and those who need and love us, every time something comes to an end... or unless we're afraid, for whatever reasons (good ones or bad), to take on new beginnings, and blame it on fate or destiny... we have to understand what's at stake. Indeed, we have to discern what we have or have not, and appreciate what we could win or lose, depending on our choices.

Then we need to do what we need to do; get ready and go.

In other words, get to work.

Getting to Work is Good.

With every new challenge, we should be better, stronger and wiser — appreciating that work takes work, and hard work takes hard work. As an added bonus, the reward for our hard work and gritty determination, will help us know so much more in many different ways, including:

- ✓ Intellectually

- ✓ Physically

- ✓ Emotionally

- ✓ Spiritually

The experience we earn, both good and bad, is never insignificant.

It's Invaluable.

As Ralph Waldo Emerson put it,

> *"When a man is pushed, tormented, defeated,*
> *he has a chance to learn something; he has been put on his*
> *wits… he has gained facts, learned his ignorance, is cured of the*
> *insanity of conceit, has got moderations and real skill."*

There's another bright side about your new life, and going to work for a living. If you think about it, you (or someone), now go from paying for school (in one way or another), to getting paid to learn. With that view in mind, it's like it is with so many of life's defining moments and how we deal with our triumphs, as well as our trials and our tribulations.

It's about:

Perspective
(how we <u>look</u> at things)

Attitude
(how we <u>feel</u> about things)

Aptitude
(how we <u>work</u> at things)

Mindfulness
(how we <u>think</u> of things)

As an acronym – that spells **PAAM**.

(Good) PAAM is Good.

Whether we choose to have the right PAAM or the wrong PAAM, is completely up to us. We're in charge. Now admittedly, there are going to be lots of people who will tell you, in effect, the same thing. Most people, especially family and teachers, mean well, and tell you these things out of kindness and love. Be that as it may, you and I both know that it's probably going to get a little old, and annoying. No doubt.

I also appreciate that you might look at some of these folks and think,

> *"What the heck do you know about it?*
> *It's easy for you to say, you're not me?!"*

That's true.

We're not.

However, everyone on the planet, including your parents, deals with issues and difficulties. At one time or another, we're all challenged with having good PAAM. Thankfully, most of us are able to take charge, persevere, and pull ourselves up by the proverbial bootstraps.

Perseverance is Good.

I know it can be done, and I'm not any stronger than you. Really. I know this because at twenty-seven, during a big low point in my life, I was living in L.A. with no job, and no money. My situation got so bad, that I sold most of my stuff just to get by, and for a period of time, lived in an unpaid apartment without electricity (which meant no lights, no TV, no fridge: talk about adding insult to injury). That was a far cry from what I thought would have been my situation at that time, having moved from Indianapolis to live a supposedly "more exciting life."

Riiiiiiiiiiiiight (not).

You see, within months after moving to California, and starting a new job, I got suddenly RIF'd (meaning "reduction in force"), which is what some companies call it when they let people go to cut costs. In other words, I got the boot; let go; the heave-ho; terminated; canned; fired.

Due to my lack of income, a mountain of debt, and a heavy dose of frustration, sadness and woeful disillusionment — my life literally and metaphorically stink, stank, stunk. To put it mildly, I did not like life.

Writing about those feelings now… knowing about all of the love, and outstanding things that are in my life today… I'm dismayed that I ever had such sad times and reckoned myself to be an irredeemable failure.

But I *was* broken: financially, emotionally, physically, spiritually.

And just too prideful (and dumb) to ask for help.

Then one day, thankfully, about four weeks into this heavy crappy funk, I was sitting in a grubby cantina, scarfing down the $3.99 all-you-can-eat buffet (me and about twenty other down-and-out bums), and it struck me, an epiphany if you will: it was time to get going! It was time to pack my bags, move on, and head back home to my family. There would be no more wallowing in self-pity, no more anger, no more tears.

It was time to reclaim life, take charge, and get going.

Giddy-Up!

So, while I moved to Los Angeles with a truckload of furniture, an abundance of youthful exuberance, and a heart-full of misguided dreams — I drove away with two small suitcases, some pictures, and whatever else could fit in my fancy sports car (a painful and expensive reminder of better paydays), which of course I could no longer afford, and would have been repossessed, if they could have found me.

Living on the run from creditors is a drag: D-R-A-G-DRAG.

What I lacked in friendship, cash and material possessions, I made up for in an invigorated attitude. I felt fine, and happy to go home ☺.

There was more good news: I had actually managed to hook up with a potential job back in Indianapolis — although it literally required me to drive across the country in two days flat. But hey, if Speed Racer could do it, I could too. Go Go Go! (That expression is from the *Speed Racer* cartoon. You know about *Speed Racer*, right? And his awesome car the Mach 5, as well as his brother in-disguise, *Racer X* (who by the way, was way cooler than Speed, and I'm not ashamed to admit it, was one of my childhood heroes, even if he was just a cartoon). But I digress.)

Anyhow, thanks to a friend who wired me some much needed cash... and fueled by warm thoughts of being reunited with my family... I was able to make it to Indy on an empty stomach, and an empty tank.

But I made it. And I even got the job.

It was an okay job, with okay pay. But it was a job, and it paid.

It afforded me the opportunity to live in a small, dumpy hotel room with a bed that folded out of the wall (just like you see in the old black and white movies). I horded my pennies, and basically ate PB&Js, soup, cereal, and mac 'n cheese for two months straight. No kidding.

But thanks to a lot of hard work, the right PAAM and a little luck...

(remember that thing about luck, and that it happens when

preparation meets opportunity)

I was able to move into a shabby apartment with rented furniture.

Long story short, I got settled and got back on track, and never really reminisced much about that challenging time — until this moment. So truly, I do appreciate the whole "it's over, and it's just begun" theme, as well as having the right (and for that matter, the wrong) PAAM.

Been there.

Done that.

Lived it.

As far as you're concerned, when you meet the next crossroads in your life (big or small), consider this: Yes, it's over. In this case, maybe your time in school, and to a certain degree — the comfort of childhood, being a kid and best-of-all, being taken care of. On the other hand, it's only just begun. An exciting and brilliant new life awaits you: the good, the bad, and yes, the ugly. And that, my friend, is absolutely awesome.

Appreciate it.

Treasure it.

Embrace it.

As the Dave Mathews song *Cry Freedom* implores,

The Future is no Place for Your Better Days.

Indeed.

Now, on a serious note, I get that sometimes the pain that comes from depression, fear, and loneliness can be excruciating and unbearable. Sadly, that type of suffering can lead to really difficult times, and even thoughts of suicide. Understanding that, if you ever hurt to the point of desperation, or if you know someone else who is or might be desperate, please seek help: and do so NOW! And do so on behalf of today's you, tomorrow's you, and all of those that do, and will, love you. Got it!?

A Chinese proverb says that a journey of a thousand miles begins with a single step. Closer to home, John Mellencamp sings two great songs, "Your Life Is Now" and "Walk Tall." Taken together, Mellencamp suggests that we need to be careful in what we assume, because there's a lot of stuff that can get us disorientated. Also, he tells us that having enthusiasm for living, along with compassion, love and forgiveness — will help us get through life's uncertainties, and disappointments.

Just remember that while you're at it, be sure to enjoy the journey.

After all,

"The Journey" $\underline{\text{is}}$ "The Destination"

Think about it.

So get stepping.

Stay safe.

And enjoy the walk.

Safe and Enjoyable Walks are Good.

CHANGE IS DIFFICULT, EVEN GOOD CHANGE

Perspective, Attitude, Aptitude, Mindfulness

"Don't cry because it's over,
smile because it happened, and will happen."

ANON

It's been said by some...
that the only certainties in life...
are change, death and taxes.

Wow, kind of a downer supposition, don't you think?

In an effort to lighten that one up, and balance out the doom and gloom, let's come up with a few light-hearted "certainties." A couple that come to my mind, are the certainties that the Chicago Cubs won't win the World Series; that I'll never get a hole-in-one, and that pigs will never actually fly (who invented that ridiculous expression, anyhow?). How about you: can you think of some "certainties" that need challenging?

You know what though, unlike pigs growing wings, I do hold out hope for the Cubbies, and making a hole-in-one, just like we in Indiana held out hope that the Colts would win the Super Bowl — and they did!

Dreams can come true: especially if we work hard, and keep the faith.

Dreams, Faith and Focus are Good.

For the sake of argument, let's agree that change is inevitable and constant. As soul singer Sam Cooke sang, "a change is gonna come." Around the same time, another famous man, John Kennedy, said,

"Everything changes but change itself; change is the law of life."

He's right, of course.

I'm also intrigued by the angle that singer Tracy Chapman takes in her emotively poetic song, "Change." In the song, she wonders that if we knew that we were going to die (unexpectedly sooner than later, of course), would we in fact change who we are, or what we've done?

Would you change?

Why would you change?

And how would you change?

Make no mistake: Our individual ability to 1) Identify, 2) Promote, 3) Manage, and 4) Live with CHANGE, and the uncertainty that it comes with CHANGE, is critical in our personal and professional lives.

With that in mind, there's this misconception that gnaws at me, so bear with me as I set the record straight. You've heard of Darwin, right? He was the dude that basically discovered evolution. The problem is, lots of folks have his theory of "natural selection" all wrong. Darwin didn't say evolution was about survival of the *strongest*; he said *survival* was all about *adaptability*. Those that are capable of adapting *evolve*.

Those that are incapable, become *extinct*.

In other words, it's not about *strength*.
It's about **adaptability**.

Unfortunately, I've known some businesspeople that have used Darwin's incorrect view to rationalize aggressive behavior, and strong-arm, bully-like tactics in business and in the workplace. Not cool.

Anyhow, if you want to learn more about how good companies evolve, adapt and grow (this book is about career-centric life skills, after all), I recommend two books by Geoffrey Moore. One is called, appropriately enough, *Dealing with Darwin*. The other is its groundbreaking predecessor, *Crossing the Chasm*. Both are really good books.

Really Good Books are Good.

Now then, what's so difficult about change?

For one thing, it can be hard and uncomfortable; whether it's good change, like getting hired, or bad change, like getting fired. Come to think of it, sometimes getting hired can be a bad change, and sometimes getting fired can be a good change.

It happens.

Change produces uncertainty, which is often accompanied by its bumpkin pals: confusion, disorientation, sadness, hostility and the ever-popular "why-the-heck-is-this-happening-to-me!?" As history's shown, and our world is still proving today in many sad and silly ways, people and society don't generally like situations that make them uneasy.

Change makes lots of people uneasy.

But what if we took a more proactive initiative to embrace change? What if we made it our friend and our ally (and do so without the use of Jedi mind tricks)? At the very least, make change make us better, not worse. Granted, that's easier said, than done. But let's do it anyway.

At least try.

Why Not?

If we think about it… feeling crummy and acting crummy because something is changing, and/or changed… is a drag. It really is. So let's not act crummy. It's draining, and a major waste of time, and energy.

Life's too short to be a mad and angry grump.

Grumps are Bad.
(So are Haters.)

At the pleasure of sounding like Mr. Rogers (by the way, Fred Rogers was an exceptional man who lived an incredible life), we should all be fans of some of the time-tested, motivational one-liners, like: "If life gives you lemons, make lemonade." "No rain, no rainbow." "You've got to break some eggs, to make an omelet." And of course, we have to appreciate the wisdom from Chevy Chase, aka Ty Webb in the movie *Caddyshack*, in that, "A flute without holes, is a stick; a donut without a hole, is a danish." (Okay, I have to admit that I used that head-scratching quote, because it's amusing, and it's from one of my favorite flicks. I also did it to make sure that you're paying attention. If you are, good. As Bill Murray, aka Carl in *Caddyshack* would say, "So I got dat goin' fer me, whichish nishe.")

The importance for us to have a positive/do-it-anyway/turn-the-other-cheek/take-the-high-road/flip-that-frown-upside-down upbeat mentality is imperative. Not convinced? Here's what Mother Teresa wrote (or at least, is given credit for) in the brilliant piece, *The Final Analysis.*

"People are often unreasonable, illogical, and self-centered. Forgive them anyway. If you are kind, people may accuse you of selfish, ulterior motives. Be kind anyway. If you are successful, you will win false friends and true enemies. Succeed anyway. If you are honest and frank, people may cheat you. Be honest and frank anyway. What you spend years building, someone could destroy overnight. Build anyway. If you find serenity and happiness, they may be jealous. Be happy anyway. The good you do today, people will often forget tomorrow. Do good anyway. Give the world the best you have, and it may never be enough. Give the world the best you've got anyway. "

Hits home, doesn't it?

Earlier, we talked about Perspective, Attitude, Aptitude, and Mindfulness (PAAM) as important elements that help us deal with change. There's a fun *Dennis the Menace* cartoon where Dennis is forced to sit in a chair facing the corner, as he was required to when he did something bad. With his mom standing behind him, fuming with anger, Dennis says, "But we'll laugh about this when we're older."

Cute, yes, but he had a point.

As a parent, as well as in my professional work, and for that matter, just going about life — I often have to remind myself of this "don't sweat the small stuff" perspective when feeling crummy in a crummy situation that, in the big scheme of things, I should just let it go.

At the very least, I need to put it into proper perspective, and just chill.

Chill is Good.

While we're using cartoons, remember back to Timon and Pumba from *The Lion King* (now don't be embarrassed, it's okay to admit that you still love the movie like you did as a kid) and their finger-snapping, toe-tapping little ditty, "Hakuna Matata," which means no worries, for the rest of your days; it's their problem-free... philosophy. Not bad advice. And I bet reading the words, also got you singing some, didn't it?

Sure it did.

Perspective

Attitude

Aptitude

Mindfulness

(PAAM)

How we choose and manage our PAAM, is up to us.

We're the navigators and drivers (for the most part).

And we're in control (for the most part).

Pearl Buck, a wonderful American novelist, wrote,

> *"Once the <u>what</u> is decided, the <u>how</u> always follows. We must not make the <u>how</u> an excuse for not facing and accepting the <u>what</u>."*

In business, as in life, it's not just how we deal with change, but also what we do with change that matters. It's about the tangibles and the intangibles. This brings us to the difference between accepting change, and creating change.

Good companies and the folks who work for them (from the president, to the receptionist), should understand and appreciate their ability, and their responsibility, to affect change. However, change for the sake of just change, without good, identifiable reasons, and whenever possible, a measurable return on investment (ROI), is bad business.

Changing and improving, are two different things.

In business, good reasons to change are because of issues related to sales and profits, competition, product innovation or obsolescence, globalization, technology, shifting trends in socio-economic behavior, bad people and bad alignment, operational inefficiencies and most of all, because of the constant, unwavering drive to do better and to do more; that is, to grow more, sell more, save more, produce more, be more and make more — in particular, more sales and profits, while at the same time, having happy customers and happy employees.

Happy Customers and Happy Employees are Good.

Bad reasons for a business to change are: appeasing over-inflated egos, incorrect assumptions, mere speculation, wishful thinking, the selfish need to create "silos" and "fiefdoms," the introduction of dumb products or unwanted services, because someone wants to hide their skullduggery (and act like they're working when they're not), and silliest of all, just because someone reads about it in a book.

(Nothing wrong with a little self-deprecating humor.)

To ensure that change is justified, and to alleviate the infamous FUD factor (which stands for fear, uncertainty and doubt), there need to be programs and processes to ensure that change is properly envisioned and that it is designed, implemented, managed, measured and adjusted in a formal and aligned fashion. We call this "**Change Management**." It's a big deal, and at least conceptually, something we should all be conversant and comfortable with, personally and professionally.

———————

Speaking of change and the unanticipated, Sherlock Holmes and Dr. Watson go on a camping trip. They set up their tent and fall asleep. Hours later, Holmes wakes his friend and says, "Watson, look up at the sky and tell me what you see." Watson replies, "I see millions of stars." Holmes then says back, "What does that tell you?" Watson ponders and then professes, "Astronomically speaking, it tells me that there are millions of galaxies and potentially billions of planets. Astrologically, it tells me that Saturn is in Leo. Time-wise, it appears to be approximately a quarter past three. Theologically, it's evident our Lord is all-powerful and we are insignificant. Meteorologically, it seems we will have a beautiful day tomorrow." After a short pause he asks, "What does it tell you?" Sherlock Holmes is silent for a moment, then says, "Watson, you idiot, someone's stolen our tent."

Now that's an example (albeit a stretched one) of reactive, "what-now" change recognition. In business, it's much better to have proactive, "what's-next" change identification. Either way, reactive or proactive, that's pretty much what change management is all about: planning for, incorporating and managing the expected, as well as the unexpected.

———————

There are many business books about change management. And there are also lots of tools to help with change management. One of the best is from the American Process and Quality Center (APQC). They have a simple chart that frames the elements of good change management.

According to APQC, effective change requires:

Vision

Skills

Incentives

Resources

Action Plan

If we can be accountable for the ownership, activity and the results of each of these... then we can effectively manage change, be comfortable with change, and hopefully get a positive result from the change... which in turn, should lead to better mojo and bigger juju (say what!?).

On the other hand, if we're missing <u>vision</u>, we'll get **confusion**.

If we're missing <u>skills,</u> we'll get **anxiety**.

If we're missing <u>incentives,</u> we'll get **gradual change**.

If we're missing <u>resources,</u> we'll get **frustration**.

And if we're missing an <u>action plan,</u> we'll get **false starts**.

Sound simple enough?

Well, it's not.

To begin with, each one of those requirements has many variables, subsets and derivatives. They can also be conflicting, especially when it comes to balancing our personal lives with our professional ones. Mix in the inevitable input, recommendations and influence from family and friends, along with a smattering of issues around politics, religion, ethics and emotions, and we end up having to deal with a lot of stuff.

That's why our ability to discover change, promote change, accept change, manage change and live with change is critical. To that end, it really helps to follow a framework like the APQC which can programmatically direct and guide us in determining, managing, inspecting and measuring ourselves.

Like in business, if we can't inspect it, we can't measure it.

If we can't measure it, then how do we know how well we're doing?

Measuring is Good.

To help get you started, let me share with you my own vision that's used to guide, drive, manage, inspect and measure my life. I actually refer to it as my vision/mission/value statement, as it includes more than just a vision, *per se*. I wrote this last version in late 2013, and depending on changes in my life, I'll update it accordingly. It goes:

> "I will strive to be a good, compassionate and loving person — doing my very best to live a gracious, giving and balanced life. I will respect and nurture my mind, body and spirit so that I can continuously appreciate, embrace, and accomplish my responsibilities as a trustworthy husband, father, son, brother, friend, colleague, neighbor and citizen. I will work hard and smart, and do what needs to be done to have a productive, enjoyable and beneficial livelihood. I will provide for and protect my family, and those who depend on me. And with God's good grace, I will live a healthy, happy, loving, family-oriented life."

There you have it, my own vision/mission/value statement.

But it's more than that actually, as it's really the foundation to "my cause/my calling." In other words, it's my "why" for doing what I do.

Whys, Causes and Callings are Good.

Here's the deal: If you do your homework and prepare, have the right PAAM, and look at change and all that comes with it as building blocks, not stumbling blocks, and as advances, not setbacks… you'll hopefully enjoy a more productive, happy and successful career.

More importantly, you'll enjoy a more rewarding life.

Earlier, I quoted Johann Goethe, the German novelist, playwright and philosopher. He also wrote an impactful little piece called the "Nine Requisites for Contented Living," and they are:

1. Health enough to make work a pleasure

2. Wealth enough to support your needs

3. Strength enough to battle difficulties and overcome them

4. Grace enough to confess your sins and forsake them

5. Patience enough to toil until good is accomplished

6. Charity enough to see some good in your neighbor

7. Love enough to be useful and helpful to others

8. Faith enough to make real the things of God

9. Hope enough to remove fears concerning the future

Goethe was a deep thinker and legend, especially in his own mind. (That was a slight dig on the fact that Mr. G had a very big ego.)

By the way, as you will inevitably change, and hopefully for the better, you should realize that those around you may not always be comfortable with your changes, even if those changes are good.

But especially if they're bad.

A few years ago, one of our new employees, straight out of college, confided in me that he was having problems getting along with his roommate and girlfriend. It turned out that their respective priorities and expectations had changed. They had conflicting PAAM.

He had big aspirations and was motivated to focus on his job and do it well, to work hard, to be a quick learner and to excel so that he could take his profession and life to the next level. He was truly passionate about business and having a good career, along with the income, fun and stability that it can generate. He even talked about buying a house, getting married, and starting a family. The roommate and girlfriend, however, wanted to party and stay out late. They were much less passionate about their jobs, professional goals, and even their future.

They were, in a word: indifferent.

As you can assuredly imagine, having such different philosophies, it inevitably got uncomfortable for all three. Our man eventually broke up with his girlfriend, moved into his own apartment, and is doing great.

So heads-up: relationships can, and will, change as you change.

But you know that already, don't you?

That said, don't sweat it if you can't be the person you want to be today, or next month, a year from now, or ever, for that matter.

But keep trying. Every day.

Progress is an **evolution**, not a **revolution**.

And for the record, it's important to note that just because I write about progress, and am fairly comfortable with it given my background — it doesn't mean I have it all figured out. I'm still flawed; just ask around.

Indeed, I have work to do.

Everyday.

Just like you.

Kapish?

But improve we can, and improve we will.

As Edgar Allen Poe wrote,

"I have great faith in fools. My friends call it self-confidence."

Another scholarly dude by the name of Oscar Wilde wrote,

"Every saint has a past, and every sinner has a future."

Speaking for myself, those are both good to know.

Self-Improvement is Good.
(and always possible)

THERE'S NO SUCH THING AS ENTITLEMENT

Work Takes Work;
Need to Earn What We Get

"To be is to do."

Let's assume you were born sometime between 1981 and 2000. (And if you're not, play along; sometimes playing make-believe, even at your age, and mine, is A-OK). Did you know that your generation is often referred to by sociologists, the media, and employers — as the "Me Generation," or "Generation Why?" and most distressing of all, the

"Entitlement Generation"

That's a pretty heavy word, *entitlement*.

And in this case, as it relates to "you guys," not exactly flattering.

So how do those labels make you feel?

My guess is, not too happy.

Right or wrong, your generation is often considered by (too) many as being ungrateful, impatient, coddled, dissatisfied, disinterested, immodest, materialistic, and high-maintenance. You're criticized for thinking that you're, well, you-know, entitled, to everything that hard work and its rewards have to offer — here and now, without having to work for it. Sure, this is a generalization, but it's what "they're" saying.

Don't believe it?

Well, take a look at how Ms. Oprah Winfrey described her frustration with today's "entitlement generation." As the story goes, she donated loads of money to build schools in South Africa (instead of the United States), and rationalized that her main reason for doing so was because, as she put it, "If you ask the kids [in the U.S.] what they want or need, they will say an iPod or some sneakers. In South Africa, they don't ask for money or toys. They ask for uniforms, so they can go to school."

OUCH!

Talk about guilty by association. She doesn't even know you personally, yet she, and too many other folks, are disappointed with your entire generation. It's a shame when your cards are stacked against you, even before you get a chance to prove the critics and naysayers wrong.

Now, I actually think Oprah is a good woman, on many levels. Clearly she's very giving, charitable and smart; but she really took a shot at our Millennial generation. That's why some people, me included, are sure there was more on her agenda. Maybe Dr. Phil had her doing some reverse psychology to motivate us to step up and fix the attitudinal problems between our generations, or help bridge the generational gap.

For what it's worth, there are a lot us who are not giving up on you, or your generation. No way. Never. In fact, there are actually millions and millions of people wanting to help you and your peers, deal with and overcome some of the obstacles and challenges that you're facing.

We call them **family**.

But keep in mind that as family, we can only do so much. At the end of the day, we're not going to do your job, let alone live your life, for you.

We can only assume that nobody else will, either.

Personal Responsibility is Good.

That's our way of saying that you shouldn't look for or expect preferential treatment. For the most part, you're on your own. At your age, only you can get yourself out of bed in the morning, and put yourself to bed at night. In between, only you can choose the right values, behavior and manners that you want to live by. You alone.

Clearly, there are some very real (and troublesome) factors that contribute to whole this entitlement dilemma. That said, while I'm not one of those goofs who think that today's "popular culture" is the root of all evil (just some of it)… I do believe that we need to be careful of what culture we consume, or at the very least, how we consume it.

Let's take certain television for instance.

I'm particularly miffed with programs like *Jersey Shore* and *The Real World* (a more appropriate title for both shows would be *Absurdsville: Lifestyles of the Totally Spoiled and Dysfunctional*), which encourage superficiality and entitlement, and are enormously effective in doing so.

> Yeah, I think they're a problem.
> But that's just me.

(I know… I'm not supposed to be a hater; but I do hate those shows.)

Anyhow, for the sake of time, let's not go there completely. Suffice it to say, I think *sensationalist* shows that promote **elitism, decadence, debauchery, instant gratification**, and **entitlement**… are setting up a lot of young people for potential trouble, and a harsher reality down the road.

Harsh is Bad.

Here's something Bill Gates, the founder of Microsoft (and the world's richest man), said to a class of students. Specifically, he spoke about how today's feel-good, everyone-gets-a-trophy-whether-you-win-or-lose mindsets, are creating a generation of kids with a poor concept of reality. That fact… coupled with some indifferent, give-them-whatever-they-want parenting, as well as the kid's own unrealistic expectations… is setting them up for disappointment, frustration and failure.

> He sees it daily.

According to Mr. Gates:

1. Life is not fair. Get used to it.

2. The world won't care about your self-esteem. The world will expect you to accomplish something BEFORE you feel good about yourself.

3. You will NOT all make forty thousand a year right out of high school. You won't be a vice president... until you earn it.

4. If you think your teacher is tough, wait 'til you get a boss. They don't have tenure.

5. Flipping burgers is not beneath your dignity. Your grandparents had a different word for burger flipping: they called it opportunity.

6. If you mess up, it's not your parents fault, so don't whine about your mistakes, learn from them.

7. Before you were born, your parents weren't as boring as they are now. They got that way from paying your bills, cleaning your clothes and listening to you talk about how cool you are. So before you save the rain forest from the parasites of your parents' generation, try delousing the closet in your own room.

8. Your school may have done away with winners and losers, but life has not. In some schools, they have abolished failing grades, and they'll give you as many times as you want to get the answer. This doesn't bear the slightest resemblance to ANYTHING in real life.

9. Life is not divided into semesters. You don't get summers off, and very few employers are interested in helping you find yourself. Do that on your own time.

10. Television is not real life. In real life, people actually have to leave the coffee shop and go to jobs.

11. Be nice to nerds. Chances are you'll work for one.

What do you think?

Does the tag "entitled" resonate with you or people you know?

At the very least, there's probably some "guilty by association," right?

Ready to do something about it?

Understanding and being understood, has a lot to do with what we call **Emotional Intelligence**. If possible, everyone, along with their family, should own a copy of *The Art of Living: The Classical Manual on Virtue, Happiness and Effectiveness*, by Sharon Lebell. My sister gave me this book a few years back, and it's one of the most brilliant books to help with emotional intelligence. *The Art of Living* is Lebell's interpretation of the stoic philosopher, Epictetus. Although Epictetus lived in A.D. 55, his views are remarkably modern and inspirational. If you had just one book that could easily fit in your backpack, or by the side of your bed — I would recommend that one. Trust me. Go get it.

One of the greatest contributing factors to the entitlement mentality today, is, I'm sad to say, parents. The conventional assumption is that many parents need to do a better job (when appropriate) of saying, something to the effect of, "I love you, but no, you can't have everything you want, when you want it. No, you can't just slouch around, wear and say whatever you want and expect us to just give you money. No, you can't act like a punk, or spoiled, or bossy or get in trouble without consequences. And absolutely yes, I do love you, and that's why I say no. In other words, I say no because I love you."

At the same time, most parents can also do a better job of praising as appropriate, and helping to build humble self-confidence. For sure.

Granted, there are plenty of real and not so real generalizations about lackadaisical parenting. Regardless, many parents, including me, need to do a better job at saying no, and sticking to it… even if it means having to upset our kids… or shake the proverbial family tree.

If you think about it — isn't it really astonishing how such a small, simple, straightforward, matter-of-fact, two-letter-word like

No

… can be so incredibly challenging, sensitive and difficult.

No isn't always bad.

Here's a quick break suggestion: put the book down; walk away; grab yourself a snack (a glass of cold milk and some Oreo cookies sounds good, but that's just me), and go Google "Entitlement Generation."

Go ahead. Check it out. Don't worry; I'll be here when you get back.

Soooooo (insert awkward pause here), what do you think?

Accurate?

Off the mark?

In the ballpark?

Regardless, I get the feeling that you probably want to tell all of us has-been, old-schoolers that we don't get it, and to get off your back.

The problem and the reality are though — that you can't, and if you do, you shouldn't — because we're your parents, bosses and colleagues.

For a lot of reasons, and I'm not saying that they're correct or justified, but you have to accept these generalizations, and work from there.

Sure, you can be upset and say it's not fair, because it's just not you. But only you (and maybe others who know you better) recognize that. And if you're looking for someone's opinion as to your specific situation, just be careful of asking those who truly love you. Because sometimes, those that truly love you just don't see what they don't want to see, or they accept you because they love you, unconditionally.

As they say, love's blind.

————————

Let's return to parents, and parenting.

While it's nice to love unconditionally, it's not so great to parent unconditionally. Parents sometimes have to be subjective and objective. Parenting is a real job, and like all jobs, it can be uncomfortable, and it's not always fun. Sometimes we have to do things that we don't want to do, like if necessary, having to treat our own children under the same demands and expectations that employees face, i.e. proper time and attendance and work habits. And we don't do this under the auspices of "tough love" — but for real love, and for our mutual lifelong benefit.

Good Parenting is Good.

The generalization about you being the "Entitlement Generation" is not going to change anytime soon. It is what it is, and will be for some time. That said, most philosophies/philosophers tell us that we should accept inappropriate stigmas... and consider our challenges, obstacles and even the difficult people and difficult situations that we inevitably encounter... as lessons from which to learn, and improve ourselves.

Now, while I embrace that thinking for the most part, I am not a believer, fan or an advocate in Nietzsche's flawed and problematic philosophy that says: "What doesn't kill us makes us stronger." Because more often than not, it doesn't make us stronger, it makes us weaker. Again, sadly, too many parents and too many companies use that inappropriate thinking to rationalize over-aggressive treatment.

Ugh, not good.

Speaking of pop culture, and trying to look at things in a different manner — the other night on a run, I (just so) happened to hear that old Dixie Chicks song, "Not Ready to Make Nice." It's a powerful tune. I appreciate the passion, instrumentation, and vibe. If you listen to the lyrics and know the story behind the song, you can understand why the lead singer, Natalie Maines, is so impassioned about its message.

After all, we should all support the right to (intelligent) free speech, and like her, be disheartened that especially in the U.S., speaking your mind (assuming that you're not spewing racism, terrorism, hatred or bigotry) can generate loathing and death threats. Undeniably, it's also a shame that a mother would ever teach her daughter to hate an innocent stranger. Worse yet, that someone would threaten to kill that stranger just for having a different opinion about another person. Shameful.

(By the way, doesn't everyone, regardless if you're a Democrat, Republican, Independent, or just an old wet blanket, detest war? Sure, there can be rationale to be in war, such as fighting for right reasons, especially defending ourselves from the bad guys, and protecting those that need protecting. But it doesn't change the fact that war is dreadful.)

War is Sad.
War is Bad.

If it was my song though, I'd keep most of the lyrics, but I'd like to change the title to "Ready to Make Peace." The message remains the same, but the goal changes. Natalie espouses that thinking herself when she talks about wanting to forgive, but not necessarily forget.

Forgiveness is Good.

The forgiveness doctrine worked well for Gandhi, Martin Luther King, Mother Theresa, and Jesus — not a bad group to emulate. So I ask myself, what would they do if misinterpreted, persecuted or wronged?

Would they stomp their feet and shout injustice?

Would they get angry and look for a fight?

Would they give up and quit?

I can't help but think they would put it into proper perspective, take the right stand, and accept the name-calling for what it is. And we should all do the same in similar situations, as this name-calling issue is not exclusive to the "Entitlement Generation." This is inclusive of us all.

In any event, there's no doubt that we can all be better: better friends, colleagues, bosses, politicians, accountants, CEOs, doctors, lawyers, waiters, pilots, stockbrokers, cooks, truckers, athletes, coaches, employees, brothers, sisters, sons, daughters, mothers, and fathers.

You get the picture.

Maybe you're thinking how hard it is to take the high-road, to turn-the-other-cheek and to forgive, especially at times when it seems like such a dog-eat-dog-world, and that we're all wearing Milk Bone underwear (that's an oldie but goodie line from Norm, in the TV show *Cheers*).

As sportsman and humanitarian Arthur Ashe said,

> *"To achieve greatness, start where you are.*
> *Use what you have. Do what you can."*

Speaking of doing, let's talk about the differences between:

Realism

&

Idealism

To be a good realist, we need to be pragmatically idealistic.

To be a good idealist, we need to be fundamentally realistic.

It's like a hand-and-glove allegory, with the hands representing realism, and being the basis for the gloves, which represent idealism. Without hands, there is no need for gloves. Sure, we can have beautiful gloves, but by themselves, doing nothing, even with great intentions and hope of being used, are just empty gloves. Until placed on the hands, they're mere dreamers with good intent, looking for a noble cause; aspirations unfulfilled, until they can validate their ultimate purpose of warming hands. Inversely, when it's cold (and more often than not the world is, metaphorically speaking, cold), the hands, for the most part, can go it alone. But why should they? That's what gloves are for: to keep us safe, warm and comfy.

Safe, Warm and Comfy are Good.

As you can tell, I took some real liberty with that one. Make no mistake though, my point is sincere, and matter-of-fact: We need to know the differences and synergies between idealism and realism. At times they're aligned, but more often than not, they're not. That's why we embrace both, separate and united. As the Robert Frost saying goes,

"Good fences make good neighbors."

This realism/idealism dilemma makes me think about the quotation (and literally, one of the most quoted quotations) from theologian Reinhold Niebuhr:

"God, grant me the serenity to accept the things I cannot
change, the courage to change the things I can,
and the wisdom to know the difference."

Let's get back to this whole entitlement thing.

On the bright side, there are lots of positives that are attributed to your generation, like being goal-oriented, smart, energetic, passionate, caring, innovative, creative, respectful, hopeful, and without a doubt, more tech savvy and more astute than any previous generation. Also, because your generation is so linked (wirelessly) through the use of the Internet, social media and mobile devices… you're recognized as being more connected to family and friends than previous generations.

Careful though, as high-tech can't replace high-touch. The more we embrace technology, the more we need to make sure we don't lose our human touch, and the more we need to live life together, in person.

You feel me?

By the way (and I'm sure you know this already, but maybe not to the degree that you should) – but you need to be very, very careful that you don't mess up your future by posting inappropriate material on social media, and social networking sites (and you know which ones I mean).

While it might be fun (and theoretically cool: not) to post stuff where you can rant, rave and share explicit information, just keep in mind that employers can (better still, just assume that they will) check you out on social media, if they can. Once you post your private life and personal information on the web, it's no longer private, or personal. It's not.

No doubt, this reality might not be fair or right, but that's the way it is. Today and beyond. It's really a no-brainer: Don't post content on the web that might mess up your prospects for getting hired, or encourage your employer to set you up to be fired. Just. Don't. Do. It. Period.

Technology can be good.
Technology can be bad.

Where does all of this commentary leave us? Well, here's where it leaves us — in summation, the cold hard truth, take it or leave it, fight it or make peace with it, rally with it or just do with it what you will.

The simple truth is, drum roll please…

There's no such thing as <u>entitlement</u>.

Sure, it's just a word, and the word has several meanings. True enough, given appropriate justification, there are those in the world who are entitled to some entitlement, just not you right now. Nope. So unless you hit the lottery (unlikely), or get the chance to live forever in MTV's *Real World*, complete with those beautiful, whiny, over-sexed, over-boozed, attention-seeking twenty-somethings (once again, unlikely) — you're going to have to make it by earning it: The Right Way.

But you know that already, yes?

Hey, who doesn't want to live in a cool house, with cool toys, in a cool city; partying all the time, hanging out in hot tubs, and sleeping in; working in Betty Crocker, out-of-the-box, ready-bake jobs that don't really matter; being pampered by film crews looking for "reality." We may want it, even covet it. But it's not real. That's make-believe. That's nonsense. To borrow from the songstress Gwen Stefani, that's bananas,

B-A-N-A-N-A-S.

While I believe in lending a helping hand, and that parents' should take wonderful care of their kids physically, mentally, spiritually and emotionally, I think there's a wavy line between helping and hurting, especially when it's time for our kids to enter the fulltime workforce.

For the sake of healthy dialogue and healthy debate, let's assume that you're "spoiled" (for the lack of a better word) from entitlement today, and that you get some stuff and preferential treatment that you haven't really worked for, or don't really deserve, especially at your age. Well, it's probably for the wrong reasons, and inappropriate. Sooner or later, it'll backfire, and more often than not, it'll do more harm than good.

So if you're getting by because of your family's wealth, connections or misplaced love, here's a tip: just don't get too comfortable.

Remember what we said earlier about change?

The fact is, if we want something:

WE HAVE TO WORK FOR IT

With our body, mind, heart, soul and gritty determination.

WE HAVE TO EARN IT

Through work, time, and real accomplishments.

WE HAVE TO STOMACH IT

Because it can be frustrating, and not always fun.

As I hope you know by now, I'm not here to be some finger-wagging, foot-stomping, preachy pontificator, ranting on his bully pulpit (what the heck's a bully pulpit, anyhow?), trying to tell you what to do (that ain't cool; that ain't me). And though I don't know you personally, I do respect, appreciate and admire you, as well as what you're doing; what you're going to do, and what you're going through. I honestly do.

Empathy is Good.

That said, it's all about helping you:

Learn more; be more; do more; make more.

Get, keep and excel at your job/career.

Enjoy healthy relationships.

Have a loving family.

Achieve success.

Be happy.

Success

&

Happiness

Are Good

(Don't You Think!?)

WE'RE A PERPETUAL WORK IN PROGRESS

There's Just No Room for Complacency

"Thoughts lead on to purposes; purposes go forth in action;
actions form habits; habits decide character;
and character fixes our destiny."

TYRON EDWARDS

I'll always remember the most intriguing question that was asked, during my time as Entrepreneur in Residence at Indiana University.

The question was, "**How complete are you**?"

(I know, that's just, like, so, Jerry Maguire.)

Now, before you get the answer, keep in mind that I focused our conversations on reality, change and attitude. You remember my whole "It's over, and it's just begun" mantra, don't you? Of course, you'll also recall that my message was about the importance of being humble yet confident, calm yet aggressive, working hard and working smart, understanding that failure is an event, not a sentence, and knowing that nothing ventured means nothing gained. Moreover, that we're all a perpetual work in progress, so we shouldn't sweat the fact that we don't know what we don't know, and that we aren't necessarily where we want to be. Friedrich Nietzsche (the "what-doesn't-kill-you" guy) said,

"Those who would learn to fly one day must first stand and
walk and run and climb and dance; one cannot fly into flying."

Progress is Good.

In any event, my answer was (drum roll please):

57.5%

How'd I come up with that number? Well, I did the math.

The way I figured it, I'd already lived at least one-third of the average life expectancy for a man (which in the U.S., is around seventy five, although I'm signed up for making it to ninety). I was also hoping to catch the students by surprise, especially those who were actually listening. Mostly, I really wanted them to think. And they probably did think. Specifically, they probably thought that it was a funky number, and shockingly low for a guy who's undoubtedly got a good ego, and probably believes that he's smarter than the average bear (ouch, talk about a self-inflicted wound).

Anyhow, when it was all said and done, my goofy answer generated some quizzical looks, a smattering of buzz, and with a little playful give-and-take, we had a lot of fun with it. "Show me the money!" (Sorry, I couldn't help myself; just had to go there, given the whole Jerry Maguire thing.)

So, if I was 57.5% at thirty five, what am I at forty seven?

After careful consideration and deliberation, I'm going with 68%.

And maybe if I keep applying myself, I'll get to 90% by ninety.

At least I hope so.

What about you?

How complete are you?

And don't do the mortality math, because as a young professional adult, the math's basically immaterial. That really shouldn't be a factor yet, at least not one you should needlessly worry about — at least I hope not.

What I'm asking is this: How aware and honest are you with respect to who you are now, versus who you want to become? And be real, okay?

Then there's another tough part — getting from here to there, because you just don't know what it is you want, what it is that you have to do, what it will take, how long it will take, or even if you'll get there. Buddha said, "What we think, we become." Maybe we should all think more intently about what we want to become, while realizing that we'll never actually get there, completely. We should all believe that we're a perpetual work in progress. Hopefully we embrace that reality, using that as motivation to improve and get better.

Refining is Good.

In a previous chapter, I talked about change and about leveraging the APQC framework for managing change. Here's a similar "stractical" approach, using the image of a house to help us think about our goals, progress and perpetual self-improvement as they pertain to our aspirations for our mind, body and spirit. By the way, "stractical" is a perfectly acceptable hybridization of the words **strategic** and **tactical**. Maybe it'll catch on, and maybe I should trademark it? (Remind me to call my lawyer.)

Symbolically, we can use the image of a house to help establish, identify, improve, and measure us as individuals (as you've inevitably noticed on the cover, there's a "blueprint" theme after all, right).

But we should do more than just imagine this house in our mind; we should document it on paper so that we can chart and measure our progress with how we're managing ourselves and our priorities.

Now, taken out of context, focusing on yourself like this, might seem self-centered. At the very least, it might sound somewhat self-absorbed.

Not so.

The fact is, we can't provide for ourselves and our families — let alone be good sons, daughters, parents, husbands, brothers, friends, neighbors, employees, or any of those things — without a sincere, structured, matter-of-fact, genuine self-awareness. Nope. Can't do it.

> The more (constructively) self-aware we are,
> the better we can serve and be others-oriented.

Self-Knowledge

is the beginning of

Self-Improvement

Make no mistake, there's a very big difference between being self-aware, self-absorbed and selfish. As Abraham Lincoln said, *"Always bear in mind that your own resolution to success, is more important than any other thing."* And have you been taught Lincoln was selfish?

Back to our metaphorical crib.

The foundation of our house is anchored by four walls that represent:

mind, body, spirit, values.

On top of the foundation is the first floor, which is just one big room dedicated to <u>family</u>. The second floor has four more rooms assigned to <u>work</u>, <u>finance</u>, <u>administration</u> and last but not least, <u>leisure</u>. Securely on top of our house is the roof, signifying our overarching responsibility to provide for, comfort and protect everyone who needs our help.

It's a modest house, but its home.

Home is Good.

So now, how do we determine our priorities, motivations and rationale for our foundation of mind, body, spirit and values?

To begin with, from a <u>mind</u> perspective, that's where everything starts, stops or gets hung up. We can't be anyone or do anything if we don't put our mind to it. As they say, mind-over-matter. We need to feed our minds, and one of the best ways to feed our minds, is to **read**.

Read. Read. Read.

I implore you to read voraciously, with a committed purpose to really reading, not just to pass the time or go through the motions. Take the time to read, whether you're reading fact or fiction, magazines, newspapers, cereal boxes, pamphlets handed to us on the street corner, and writing on the bathroom wall.

When we find it, we should read it; whether we agree with it, or not. In fact, that's one of the most important reasons to read everything: to challenge what we believe as we assimilate an author's opinions, ideology and philosophy.

Think about it: If we only read what we're comfortable with today... or what we're told to read because "that's just the way we think, and that's just the way it is..." then how can we ever hope to be sympathetic, or at least empathetic, to viewpoints other than our own? What if they're right, or just partially right? What if? We'll never know what we might need to know, or should know, if we don't try.

That's called willful ignorance.

IGNORANCE **IS** STUPID

On the other hand, if we don't want to be ignorant, and instead choose to understand and experience new things... the best and the cheapest way... other than being on the job or there in person... is by reading.

Reading is Good.

Another great way to feed our minds is to **listen**, and listen genuinely.

This one's not always easy, because unlike reading — where it's really only one person doing the reading — the ability to listen in the give-and-take of a conversation requires much more work. You see, reading uses just the brain, eyes, and maybe the hands. (Okay, sometimes we move our lips while reading silently, and it can be kind of embarrassing when busted; but it's not a crime.) Good listening, on the other hand, requires a lot of energy and focus, unless we're just listening to the TV, music or movies. I'm talking about in-person listening, which requires the brain, ears, eyes, mouth and body. It requires "presence," even when not personally present, like when we're on the phone.

Often, listening can be uncomfortable, because good listeners listen first and foremost to whatever the speaker has to say, whether we like it or not. That's called **active listening**. Then we talk. In between listening and talking, we think. Concurrent to listening, talking and thinking, we express interest through our presence, *vis-à-vis* our eyes, mouth, posture and hands. That's **body language**.

We use active listening and body language to show the speaker that we care, and that we are actually listening. No doubt – that's easier said, than done (especially if the other person's a loud bossy motor mouth).

Listening is hard.

Our ability to listen is either an attribute, or a detriment.

I can't overemphasis the importance of good listening — and being recognized, appreciated, and known as a good listener. There's an old adage about why God gave us two ears and one mouth, implying that we should listen twice as much as we talk. Being perceived as a poor listener is a hard label to overcome, just like it is with most labels.

So be known as a good listener.

More importantly, really be a good listener.

Do it for you, and do it for others.

Listening is Good.

A third way to improve our minds, is by **trying new things**, **meeting new people** and **seeing new places**... as well as through **writing, prayer** and **meditation**. (One of my favorite books on meditation, is called *Zen Training* by Katsuki Sekida. Check it out.)

We also improve our minds by doing the daily stuff that we take for granted, like spending time with family and friends, listening to music, playing sports, fixing something, working out, cooking, and yes, even the ho-hum things like vacuuming and doing the dishes.

You know, as a busy adult, I now understand and appreciate why my dad enjoyed washing the dishes. As a kid, it never made much sense to me. Every night when he was home, he would do the dishes, quietly and deliberately. Now, every night that I'm home, I do them as well. For one, this is because I am my father's son, and proud to be. Two, this is because it's a great time to think and reflect.

Thinking and Reflection are Good.

Mentally, we should strive to do everything that we can to make our minds better, with the ultimate, never-ending pursuit for wisdom, virtue, and peace-of-mind. Don't get me wrong: information, smarts, knowledge, know-how, skills, trades, common sense and general competencies are important. While they're good as individual assets, they're even better when leveraged collectively, because that's when we can start to approach wisdom, virtue and peace-of-mind.

From a <u>body</u> perspective, our goal should be fairly simple:

Be healthy.

Being stronger and having a few more pounds of muscle, and a few less pounds of fat is the ideal, and if that motivates you, have it. Use what you need to use to help you be healthy. Just don't go overboard and get all narcissistic. Again, the objective to being healthy is to really be able to enjoy life, with all its splendors, and yeah, its trials and tribulations.

Therefore, we need bodies that work.

That means controlling what we can control.

As you know, we can all choose to behave in ways that are healthy, unhealthy, or even down right destructive. No one can actually force us to gorge on fattening foods and become obese. (Although the way some parents feed their kids, it makes me wonder.) And no one can legally force us to smoke, take illegal drugs, drink and drive, practice unsafe sex, dive into the shallow end of the pool, and reenact the stupidity from the *Jackass* movies (don't forget why they call it "Jackass").

Granted, we can be inflicted by health issues that we cannot control. Cancer, depression, psychosis, diseases, sickness and sudden, unexpected deaths do indeed happen. Sadly, they happen way too often.

That's why it's important to appreciate the gift of life and our bodies, and to treat both with respect and love. Go on, give yourself a hug.

So let's control what we can. Stay fit and don't sweat what we can't do. After all, we're the boss of our bodies (for the most part) — so be the boss, and be a great one. And remember, while we make our own choices, those choices end-up making us. Think about it.

Healthy is Good.

From a spirit and spirituality standpoint, I don't just mean being religious, and practicing the tenets and/or written doctrines of a core religion. Additionally, we don't always have to see eye-to-eye with everything that our "inherited" religion says, or does. We should also be able to enjoy aspects, elements and mindsets of all religions. No?

Spirituality is about having a higher aspect to life, above and beyond the physical world and the here-and-now. While I personally believe in

God and Jesus Christ, and do what I can to live life as a (flawed) Christian, I also believe in additional spiritual guidance and motivation.

And yes, I think God and Jesus are good with that. Time will tell.

In my opinion, religion isn't black and white, right or wrong, we're in or we're out, we have it or we don't. Our spirit is what we make of it, and what it makes of us, in our own definition (assuming that you are capable of making that call — which you are of course, aren't you?).

In other words, and again in my own opinion, I think spirituality doesn't have to come in a one-size-fits-all, prescribed, prepackaged formula or in just one book. I think it can be an amalgamation of many.

At the end of the day, I think spirit is an intangible, ever-present aspect to our body and life that helps motivate, guide, comfort and inspire us.

Spirituality is Good.

If you want to read a provocative and compelling book that can help you better understand the religions of the world, including Christianity, Islam, Judaism, Buddhism and Hinduism, check out *Religious Literacy; What Every American Needs to Know — And Doesn't,* by Stephen Prothero. And another wonderful book that leverages, mixes and promotes spirituality from diverse religions, check out *Awareness: The Perils and Opportunities of Reality,* by Anthony De Mello.

From a values perspective, I'm talking about more than just being ethical, as we all agree that we shouldn't lie, cheat, steal, perjure, physically injure let alone kill another, or do anything that's actually illegal or against the law, at least not intentionally, or without a very good cause — like speeding and running red lights to get your pregnant wife to the hospital.

More than just for being ethical and obeying the laws of society, values pertain to how we treat people, and how we behave. To that point, values are also about kindness, generosity, compassion, courtesy, respect, listening, being a good communicator, as well as those "nice" traits that help us be better people, and moreover, better people-people.

Maintaining our values is especially tough when we work in the all-too-often combative, fast-paced, short-fused, get-the-job-done, polarizing corporate world, where trust can be hard, support convenient and styles gruff and unfriendly. And for all the wrong reasons, there's sometimes a misguided attitude in some businesses that nice folks finish last.

Wrong. Wrong. Wrong. Wrong. Wrong. Wrong. Wrong. Wrong. Wrong. Wrong. Wrong. Wrong.

Nice businesspeople, and for that matter, nice companies, can/must succeed. And the good news is, most companies want nice <u>and productive</u> employees; they really do, whether you believe it or not.

But here's the deal: because we're nice and gravitate toward likable, people-friendly, team-oriented, collaborative environments — that just means that we have to consistently work hard, perform, and execute.

Moreover, we can't act like fools, tolerate fools or accept a fool's errand. Don't be a pushover, and we won't get pushed over. Our niceness can't be taken advantage of. We do what we say, and say what we'll do. Most of all, we meet or exceed expectations, and we consistently deliver proof-positive results, with a smile and good cheer.

I'll talk more about this later and provide recommendations that can help you succeed. For now, just keep in mind that you should be a nice person, and that nice people prefer to work, befriend, defend and hang out with other nice people. (Have I mentioned that haters are bad?)

And nice people don't emulate jerks, even if they're powerful. They're still jerks, who'll often say that nice people don't have what it takes, the "killer instinct," to get the job done. In reality, they don't have what it takes, because they're one-dimensional and afraid. More often than not, they're intimidated by nice people who get things done, the nice way.

Jerks… and their fraternal order of crony cronies, including: bullies, schmucks, tyrants, tormentors, backstabbers, and all other jerk-like labels… just plain stink. Sure, they can maybe do their jobs, and maybe even get results. But do you want to work for them if given a choice?

Not.

Companies often use the word cancer (very inappropriately), to make a point about a specific problem. That said, jerk behavior and management by intimidation are cancerous. The real bummer is when the senior leaders themselves patronize, praise, promote, condone or encourage jerk behavior. That means that they're either quietly complicit, active proponents, or asleep at the wheel. This is all bad. By being indifferent to poor behavior, they're basically supporting it. Anything can be rationalized if you want it bad enough. With regard to rationalized bad behavior, I guess it's true what Upton Sinclair wrote, *"It is difficult to get a man to understand something, when his job depends on not understanding it."* That happens, and way too often.

So heads-up! When you work in a company that treats you like an animal or a prisoner, it's a problem. And when there are no guards to watch over the guards, or worse yet, when the warden is the chief villain — you have to grin and bear it, serve your time, hang in there, do your job and do it well, irrespective of the treatment… because you need the work, and it pays the bills that need paying. C'est la vie, oui.

Oh, one last thing (as if I haven't said enough on this one): Just always remember that jerks, tyrants and their entire stinky rotten posse can occasionally disarm you with insincere friendship and artificial support.

As they say, don't be duped by a wolf in sheep's clothing. On that note, you also need to beware of sheep in wolf's clothing; that happens too.

When I think about that last cliché (and its friend), I'm reminded about the famous parable of the scorpion and the bullfrog. It goes like this:

There's this nice bullfrog, working diligently on the shore. Along comes a scorpion and he asks the fine frog if he could give him a ride across the pond to the other side. The frog, being no dummy, said, "But you are a scorpion. If I get too close to you, let alone give you a ride, you will surely sting me, and I will be dead." The scorpion smiled and pretentiously responded, "Indeed, my good fellow, that may be what some other scorpions would do, but not me. In fact, I'll be your buddy; your ally. Just think how great it would be to have a scorpion to protect you and keep you safe. You can trust me. I'll do you no harm."

Interesting, thought the bullfrog. That was a pretty compelling proposition to have a scorpion in his little corner of the pond. So after a few minutes of deliberation, the frog agreed and told the scorpion to jump on his back, and they went swimming across the pond.

After getting them both safely to shore, the scorpion jumped off and immediately stung the frog. As the incredulous and gullible frog lay dying, he asked softly, "Why?" The scorpion replied without hesitation, "Because I'm a scorpion. It's my nature."

Once a scorpion…

Another "rule-of-thumb" is to stay in a job for at least two years.

Many of us have had, or still have, bad jobs, bad bosses, or work for bad companies, simply because we have to make a living. Regardless of the treatment, and assuming you're not being emotionally abused, or physically harmed — in which case, "Run Forrest Run!" — you just have to suck it up, and deal with it. While you're dealing with it, fulfill your obligations with class and good PAAM. Take the opportunity to learn from what not to do, and how not to act… so that when you do move on, you'll know better. In fact, that's how we do some of our best learning: working for and with bad bosses, colleagues and companies.

In other words, learning from what **NOT TO DO**.

As Gump said himself, "That's all I gotta say 'bout that."

Gainful employment, and getting the experience and the paychecks, are the biggest upsides. Keep in mind that no matter how bad it is, it could always be worse. It doesn't matter what your job is or who you have to work for, it has to be easier than, for example, fighting in a war.

That's why we should all be disturbed when people use military jargon, and/or war analogies, to describe business. Business isn't war, and businesspeople aren't soldiers. War is war. Soldiers get hurt and die. Let's not dishonor the courageous service and heroism of our military men and woman by ever implying an association with what they do… and the immense sacrifices they and their families make… with what happens in business, or at work. That's just wrong and disrespectful.

Disrespectful is Bad.

Speaking of (self) respect, you always have to hold your ground with regard to your own personal behavior. If you're ever in doubt or in a dilemma about acting inappropriately, try the newspaper-headline trick.

Check it out:

Picture your actions (or inactions) as headlines on the front page of your town newspaper. Would your friends and family be proud of you, buy extra copies, pass it around the coffee shop, and hang it on the fridge? Or would they be pretty disappointed, and throw it in the trash?

Here's another thing: Do us all a favor, and mind your manners.

Manners Matter.

It's both amazing and disappointing how many people, in all walks of life, can't seem to mind their manners. It's one of the first things that makes an impression, and as you undoubtedly know by now, we never get a second chance, to make a first impression, right (I'll only say that 10 more times).

Good First impressions are Good.
(lasting good impressions even better)

With regard to manners, I'm not just talking about the fact that we shouldn't act like a jerk, punk, bully, or be spoiled, smug, arrogant, scream, yell, demoralize, or belittle. Those are given assumptions.

No, I'm talking about basic niceties, like:

- Looking people directly, and intently, in the eyes.

- Proper greetings, salutations, and respectfulness, like saying hello, thank you, may I, please, no-problem, bless-you, take care, have a nice day, goodbye, after you, you're welcome, etc.

- Shaking hands with a good grip, and asking how the other is doing, with sincerity. Taking the time to authentically care.

- Being respectful of age, experience, situation and authority.

- Genuinely listening and appreciating the other side.

- Opening and holding open the door for another, or offering up a seat for someone who needs it more.

- Having good etiquette and decorum, and being mindful of our conduct while we socialize. FYI, "all-you-can-eat" buffets and "open" bars do not justify porking-out like a pig, drinking like a drunk, or saying whatever's on our mind, especially at company functions. Many careers have been messed up by indulgence.

- Dressing appropriately for the appropriate situation.

- Professional decorum, courtesy and earned respect.

- Using intelligible grammar and enunciation.

- Playing nice together, or even against each other.

- Not getting belligerent and lashing out with harsh explicatives, menacing facial expressions, and raised middle fingers over the little mistakes that we all, at one time or another, have made and likely will make again. As the saying goes: to err is human, to forgive divine. (That said, I do get relatively agitated when someone hassles me, or pushes my buttons, for no good reason. It also bothers me when people are late, drive too close to my bumper, especially when we're driving relatively fast, don't use turn signals, talk loud during movies and litter — tsk, tsk, tsk.)

- Respecting other people's time, possessions, and boundaries.

- Cleaning up after ourselves, or even after others who have the disregard not to clean up after themselves. For example, I'll wipe down the mess in a bathroom (toilet and all), even if the mess was there before me. You see, I just don't like to give the next person the impression that I created the mess, and didn't have the courtesy to clean up. Admittedly extreme and I don't like it. But I do it.

(If you like, feel free to take a break, and write down some of your own pet peeves in the space below. Have fun and be creative.)

-

-

-

-

-

-

-

All that said, we should also be huge fans of:

individualism

self-expression

personal liberties

After all, what a boring world this would be without:

uniqueness

differentiation

personal-taste

Distinctiveness is Good.

However, let's just not be fans of belligerent aggression, acting like an idiot, being juvenile, and wearing a bad attitude as a badge of honor. If you want to hang out with the wrong crowd... or think it's hip to destroy things, be mean and condescending, hurt people and talk foul-mouthed gibberish smack... that's your (bonehead) prerogative. But before you go singing that lame song, just think about the guy who sang it. (Uh, that would be Bobby Brown; you want to emulate him.)

Two more things to keep in mind.

Number one: Perception is Reality.

As much as that may be unfair, unjust and downright superficial (and I would agree with you, for the most part), that's the way that it is, especially with the people who are older than you. Seriously though, tell me that you've never looked at or talked with a stranger, whose mere appearance spoke so loudly about whom you thought they were, that you couldn't hear the content of what they were actually saying.

It happens.

Here's one of my favorite "perception-is-reality" stories:

These guys are playing golf. One of them's a real jerk. Nobody liked him. It just so happened that the jerk was bothered by bugs buzzing around his head. The other guys didn't have any problems with bugs. They were bug-free. The guy with the bugs asked if anyone had ever seen such nasty critters, to which one of the other golfers responded yes, and that they were called "circle flies," and he explained that they got their name because they fly around the backside of horses, in circles, just like they were doing to him. After a few moments the jerk looked over and said, "Hey, you calling me a horse's ass?" The guy responded, "I'm not calling you that. But you can't fool those flies."

The point is, if you act like a punk with a punk attitude, people will think you're a punk with a punk attitude. If you look like a thug, people will think you're a thug. If you come off as a problem, thinking the world owes you a great job, great pay, and all of the benefits that come from hard work, but without really working — think again.

As you know or will soon find out, when you get to the working world, it's tough enough for you just being associated with your generation's entitlement generalizations (you know, that whole "guilt by association thing")… let alone actually acting entitled, or even hinting at it.

If you want to look or act like someone that the company doesn't want you to look or act like, don't. If you have to be weird and do weird things, be weird outside of the office, in your own private life.

(Just don't post your weird stuff on the Internet.)

Net/Net: Mind yourself.

Number two: Reputation Matters.

It's hard to get past a bad reputation, especially having a reputation as a cheater, a liar or being untrustworthy. Whether the reputations are accurate or bogus, they're hard to get rid of and break away from. In life and in business, especially now for you starting a new job with a clean rap sheet, the last thing you want to do is start off on the wrong foot by cheating, lying or exaggerating. In fact, you want to do the opposite by under-selling, so that you can over-deliver. That's what's great about new jobs and working with new people — they don't have to know about your past problems. We'll talk more about expectations later as they are important in business, and for that matter, in life.

Please appreciate, respect and nurture your integrity, reputation and character. This is a lifetime commitment. I know it's not always easy to tell the truth and talk straight, and that sometimes we have to exaggerate or tell "white lies," especially when it comes to hurting or helping people's feelings. Just use your good judgment.

When in doubt, remember the newspaper headline trick.

The fact is, you can work a lifetime on being good with respect to integrity and trust, but with just one little slip-up, it can all come crashing down in an instant, a heartbeat, the snap of the fingers, a flash.

Be Careful.

As Buckaroo Banzai said in the movie <u>Buckaroo Banzai,</u>

"Wherever you go, there you are."

———————————

You see, nobody wants to end up lonely, rejected, and unwanted like Rexter, the talking dog. What's that? You've never heard about Rexter?

Well then, let's tell his tail (get it, tail versus tale; he's a dog, right).

So there's this lady who goes looking for a dog. She's thinking Golden Retriever, maybe a Lab. In her search through the paper, she finds an ad for a talking dog. "A talking dog? No such thing!" she says to herself. But there it was: a talking dog; to boot, it was a Golden Retriever. This was like a real-life Dean Koontz novel. (If you haven't read his book *Watchers*, you must. It's crazy, super, big-time fun.)

Suspiciously, she calls up the owner, and makes an appointment to stop by. When she gets there, the owner greets her at the door, with a sullen, indifferent demeanor. "Hi, I'm here about the talking dog," says the woman. "Yeah, his name's Rexter." mumbles the man. "He's in the back, sitting on the couch. You can have him if you want. No charge."

Wow, that's strange, thinks the lady. *Why would this guy want to get rid of a talking dog, if indeed it was true?* So she walks on in, goes in the back, and there's this beautiful dog, sitting on the couch, watching TV. Perplexed, she just stands there for a moment, wondering how to start a conversation with a talking dog. After a few uncomfortable moments, she says, "Ummm, are you Rexter?" Sure enough, the dog quickly looks up from the TV, stares at her enthusiastically and says, in an excited voice, "Yeah, that's me, Rexter." *Incredible*, she thinks. *Absolutely incredible.* She has to know more. "So what's your story, I mean, where, what, how did you get to be like this," she inquires.

"Well, it's a fascinating story," declares Rexter, eagerly. "You see, I was born in Romania, to a family of traveling magicians. Sensing that I had a special gift, they taught me to speak. Unfortunately, the empirical czar, Ludwig Von Munchenson, learned of my special gift, captured me, and forced me to serve in his royal secret entourage. Fortunately, when he became unexpectedly blinded by his own mis-thrown boomerang, I made a run for it and jumped on board a cruise ship headed to the United States. After we landed in New York, I finagled my way into Mathew Broderick's home, where he helped me learn English. For work, I became a bodyguard for Giuliani. That got me noticed and recruited by the FBI and placed on assignment for Bush. Don't like to talk about it, but I took a bullet for him, earned a Purple Heart, retired and moved here, to live quietly for the rest of my days."

When he was done with his incredible story, the woman stands there, motionless, absolutely amazed and visibly dumbfounded. She is truly perplexed, wondering why anyone would sell, let alone get rid of for free, a talking dog — and one with that unbelievable experience.

She goes up to the man and asks, point blank, "Why would you ever get rid of such an astonishing animal?" He rolls his eyes and says,

"Because he's a big, fat, no good, stinking liar."

(I know, that's a long way to go for that punch line. But c'mon, kinda funny, yes? Try that on your parents, and they'll laugh — you watch.)

The moral of the story (I think), is that even if you're a talking dog, but you lie like a rug, people don't want to hang out with you. You dig!?

Value your integrity.

Integrity is Good.

Lastly, from a <u>family</u> perspective, that's oh-so-important.

Family should inspire all of us to be the best that we can be. Of course, everyone's circumstances with respect to family are different. Regardless, our immediate family, along with our extended family and those that we practice familial values with, are important factors for doing what we do, as well as why we do it and how we do it.

Granted, I don't know your specific family situation. It could be great, or a real drag, or somewhere in between. Your parents could be together, or divorced. You could be married, dating or single, and be happy with it, or not. Regardless of your situation — and surely you have stuff going on, and complications to deal with — but do yourself a favor, and call home.

It will be appreciated.

Call a member of your immediate or extended family and tell them that you love them, even if it's out of your character or theirs, or even if it's embarrassing and uncomfortable. Do it anyway. Better still, if you live at home with your parents, or are married or in a happy relationship, do the same thing, but give them an earnest, warm, heartfelt hug (s), as well.

Go ahead. Do it.

Hugs are Good (and free).

You know, all this thinking gives me an idea.

Earlier, I mentioned a few TV programs that bother me. Admittedly, I picked on some surreal "reality" shows more than others — and make no mistake, Jerry Springer and his like deserve grief, as well. But here's a thought: Maybe there is a way for some of the appalling TV to make up for its imbalance between bad influence and good influence.

What if MTV, or any station for that matter, aired a positive, "edu-taining" talk show devoted to intelligent discussions about what working young professionals like you are dealing with? The program could follow a fun, conversational, laid-back, guest-oriented format. Our program would be unique, because it would be mindful of, and dedicated to, helping you level-up at work, business and life.

Our show would be structured around a formula for each day of the week, starting with the fact that we'd have live music and different bands every day! In addition to great music, on Mondays the show could be about business and business-related issues. On Tuesdays, the subject might be dedicated to the mind, and we could talk about books and such that help make us smarter, better, wiser and more aware. On Wednesdays, we'd focus on the body — staying fit, eating healthy and developing and maintaining a body built for life. Thursdays, we'll get into the spirit and values. Through courteous and objective deliberation, we'll talk about ways and perspectives that can help bring enlightenment, spirituality, peace of mind and values-based living. On Fridays, just in time for the weekend, we'd focus on family and recreation. We'll discuss everything about dealing with the dynamics of today's family; but we'll also talk about lots of other things such as sports, sex, dating, style, vacations, music, food, cooking and recreational activities that young adults want to talk about to help improve their lives and their taste.

I'm not exactly sure how many people in the United States make up the young professional bracket, but it's got to be 50 million+. Your spending power and influence are enormous, to say the least. More importantly, you are the future leaders of business and country, and we need all of you to be the best that you can be. That means taking the time to learn and listen, work hard and smart, be realistic and aware, open-minded and mindful, confident and humble, desirous and content, and all in all, be balanced.

Balance is Good.

By the way, the show doesn't even need to be on TV. That's really not the point. The point is the show's "purpose," that is, a focused and programmatic commitment to well-rounded self-improvement.

That said, commit yourself to taking the initiative to develop yourself thoroughly. If you're going to take the time to get stronger, then take the time to improve your whole entire body, all of it — inside and out.

In closing, here's a brilliant poem by Henry Van Dyke called, *Be Glad of Life*. This poem captures the essence of life; why we live, what we live for, why we pursue lifelong learning, as well as embracing the fact that we are all imperfect, and therefore, a perpetual work in progress.

Van Dyke writes:

> *"To be glad of life, because it gives you the chance to love and to work and to play and to look up at the stars; to be satisfied with your possessions, but not contented with yourself until you have made the best of them; to despise nothing in the world except falsehood and meanness, and to fear nothing except cowardice; to be governed by your admirations rather than by*

your disgusts; to covet nothing that is your neighbor's, except his kindness of heart and gentleness of manners; to think seldom of your enemies, often of your friends, and every day of Christ (sorry to interrupt, but please feel free to choose your own spiritual leaders); and to spend as much time as you can with body and spirit, in God's out-of-doors. These are little guideposts on the footpaths to peace."

Go ahead, put that one on your refrigerator, next to the pictures of your

Family

&

Friends

Family and Friends are Good

Cherish Them

THE IMPORTANCE OF PERSONAL BRANDING

Promoting You, and Your Story

*"Your brand had better be delivering something special,
or it's not going to get the business."*

Warren Buffett

Companies don't just buy products, gear or equipment, *per se*.

At least the best companies don't.

They buy solutions.

They buy solutions that fill specific needs, demands and requirements. Moreover, that the solution generates a tangible, return-on-investment (ROI), as qualified and quantified in qualitative and quantitative terms.

Guess what?
The same goes for people.

Companies hire people (and more candidly, employ talented people) — to be "human" solutions (both individually and as part of a team), that presumably can, will, and should generate a provable and timely ROI.

That's the deal.

Take it. Or leave it.

On that note, it's incredibly important that you can show and tell your "story," thereby making yourself appear (and eventually deliver), on the expectation that you can be a solution to help them get from here, to there; wherever here or there is — and do so in a way that makes them happy. And happy for them (and you), is making their business better.

Better Business is Good.

That said, and given the fact that most companies won't (strike that, can't) really know if you will ultimately prove yourself as an ROI solution until you can actually prove it… the best you can do for now, upfront, is to make them think/feel/believe that you are the right fit… and that you have what it takes to get the job done: the right way.

But how do you tell "your story," and demonstrate to them that you are the right person… without proven credentials, qualifications, references or experience… especially as it relates to the job that they're hiring for?

In other words, how do you get your proverbial foot in the door?

How indeed?

Well, a super-duper, astronomically big part of it starts with:

PERSONAL BRANDING
&
TELLING YOUR STORY

Given the never-ending issues and challenges with finding the right employees… coupled with the right or wrong concerns with regard to your age and generational generalizations (you know, all that rotten "entitlement" stuff)… the importance of you establishing, developing, monitoring and nurturing your story and your personal brand is critical.

Oh sure, you can cry cry cry/boo hoo hoo/sob sob sob/whine whine whine, all you want about how unfair this whole "perception-is-reality-and-you-never-get-a-second-chance-to-make-a-great-first-impression" truism is, all you want. But guess what? It won't do you any good.

Nope.

Complaining about it is just a waste of time, and energy.

So, instead of wasting that time and energy, put them to work.

And start now.

Start today.

Well, maybe start after you finish the book, because it's got lots of good pointers to help you do, what needs to be done. Not everything, mind you. But for the most part, should help get you on the right track.

So if you're ready, let's go.

The Big 4 "X" Factors Behind Personal Branding & Telling Your Story

Everything Matters

The first rule of thumb (heck, it's more than just a rule these day, it's more like a law), is that you have to get your head around and make peace with the fact, that everything with regard to how you represent yourself... be that in technology, words, gestures, or actions... matters. Boy does it ever. And depending on the technology, words, gestures, or actions... can help or hurt you in many profound ways. And that applies to both your online and off line representations — but especially online. So be careful. And not only does everything matter in the here-and-now, but pretty much everything you do (online and off) can be recorded for both posterity sake (as they say), and yes, legal reasons.

First (And Lasting) Impressions

From social media to personal interactions, it's a fact — right, wrong, or indifferently — that you never get a second chance, to make a first impression (let alone a great one, at that). So why not make it the best first impression, you can make it? Now, understanding that you might not know how to best represent yourself, you might want to look, learn, and emulate from those that are making good representations, and borrow from them. Spend some quality time online and off, studying the way that other professionals within your field represent themselves. In addition to the tips and pointers in this book, there are lots of books, websites, and material dedicated to making impressions. Get to work.

The Yin & Yang of Social Media

For the most part, I'm a big fan of social media. I'm an even bigger fan of "social business," i.e. companies using social-centric technologies to connect, communicate and collaborate in community with employees, clients and suppliers (aka stakeholders). With regard to your individual use of social media, just remember to mind the details, as well as your Ps & Qs. And by details and Ps & Qs, I mean watch the small stuff (i.e. word choice, spelling, grammar, etc.), as much as the big stuff (i.e. lies, libel, and anything that's inappropriate). When in doubt, don't post. Not worth it. As far as actual apps and websites go, there's no doubt that currently, **LinkedIn** is the proverbial cat's pajamas when it comes to professional branding. And even though you might still be in school, it's never too early (or too late) to join LinkedIn. I'm also a fan of **CareerScribe**, which helps you craft, develop and support your story. And to top off your professional "social platform" – I think **Twitter** is a great way to connect, watch and promote. As far as **Facebook**, **Vine**, **Snapchat**, **Instagram**, **Google+**, **Pinterest** and that type of "chatty" social media – my suggestion is to keep them for friends and family (while hopefully staying clear of the psychos), and not make them part of your personal professional branding. No need. No room. No time.

Volunteer & Participate

While the Internet and social media can connect us in so many exciting (and concerning) ways, it does not take the place of physically meeting in person, and being a part of land-based groups, clubs, and programs. In-person volunteering, business networking and general socializing are still fundamentally important to your career, and life success. It's not only a great way to meet new and interesting people who might play a role in both your personal and professional life — it's also a great way to learn styles, attributes and behaviors that you might want to emulate yourself. Just be careful to know the difference between good and bad. You'll be amazed at what happens when you hang out with the right people... or associate with the wrong. Beware of creeping meatballs.

Remember, your goal is to be seen as The Right Solution:
24/7/365
(because business is always on, and it never sleeps)

BUSINESS IS PERSONAL

Economics Wins

Know Your Company

Set the Right Expectations

Good Leaders Use Good Leadership

People, Product, Process, Planning, Profit

*"Striving for success without hard work,
is like trying to harvest where you haven't planted."*

DAVID BLY

So, let's assume that you already have a job, or are in the process of getting one now, or someday. Let's also assume that you have some particular knowledge and training that will help you within your chosen field, and profession. Remember, it's okay if you don't know much beyond your schooling, and what you were/are specifically hired to do.

You're young.

You're new.

You'll learn.

For sure, you're starting to work for a company that you've never worked for before, let alone know much about. And unless you've lied about your skills and background, then your company will more likely than not be mindful of the fact that you are, in a word, inexperienced.

No worries. After all, they knew that when they hired you.

Right? You did/will tell them the truth, yes?

For the record, this isn't the book to get into the granular details about how to perform individual work, or job functions (thank goodness, right). Also, I'm not going to get into the particulars on how companies or industries specifically operate. You can find that type of information on the Internet, and in an abundance of other books. No, what I have in mind is to talk about business from a broad-strokes perspective.

I'm going to focus on the essential and fundamental elements that every person, and every company, needs to appreciate and be mindful of. And I'm not just talking about working for small to large corporations, but also not-for-profits and home-based businesses have many of the same requirements. I'd even suggest, to a certain extent, that these elements are applicable in how we live our lives.

So here we go — most of the most (but certainly not all) fundamental expectations for any good business and/or organization with regard to strategy, economics, operations, people, management, execution and leadership, plus a few other things that we should know about.

Knowledge is Good.

Reader Beware: We're going to jump knee-deep into a mess of jargon, acronyms, and other business stuff. But don't worry, it won't be boring.

(So says me ;)

To start, let's establish the core objectives for any good organization, regardless of their focus, size, or industry. Let's do this by using an introduction letter from the Chief Executive Officer (CEO), and let's call the company, Level-UP, Corp. (Hey, it's my book, after all.)

So, the CEO of Level-UP, Corp., is writing you a letter to welcome you onboard. In doing so, she's setting the stage for what she thinks about, and hopes that you'll think about as well. Let's see what she has to say.

Dear [Insert Your Name Here],

Hello and welcome aboard.

The fact that you are here at Level-UP, Corp., confirms that you're a capable, talented and trustworthy person. After all, we only hire the best. With that in mind, I'm writing to express my gratitude and enthusiasm for you joining our organization. My only regret is that I can't immediately meet with you in person.

Over time, however, we'll have the opportunity to get acquainted. In the meantime, allow me to share some thoughts on our collective responsibilities and mutual commitments at Level-UP.

To begin with, there are two priorities to always be mindful of:

> *1) **Keep Momentum**: Continue to leverage, promote and enhance the good work that we are doing today to deliver on our value proposition and our commitments, in order to generate customer satisfaction and profitable revenues.*

> *2) **Drive Progress**: We will continuously enhance our company with new strategies, products, services, resources, effectiveness and support necessary to meet or exceed our objectives for growth and profitable revenues.*

We are a high-performance, hard-working, values-based organization. We know how to innovate, acclimate and make progress quickly — thanks to our collective experience, energy and aptitude. We believe in superior teamwork and alignment. Although we manage by measurable numbers, using standardized processes, we're also adept with change and uncertainty.

With our collective knowledge, coupled with a friendly, "roll-up-our-shirt-sleeves" style, we're committed to effective execution through collaboration, accountability and trust.

We're recognized for our integrity and good governance with:

- *Balance Sheet and P&L management*

- *Operational excellence, efficiency and productivity*

- *Delivering a valued suite of products and services*

- *Managing risks and controlling costs*

- *Responsibly growing revenues and profits*

- *And we do all of this with speed, fun, great customer service, quality and a team-oriented, people-friendly, can-do attitude*

From a philosophical, "point-of-view" perspective, we believe in being a socially responsible business: dedicated to developing and supporting great solutions (and great customers), as well as the enhancement of our community. This duality of purpose, re: running a successful business, coupled with helping others in our community — is both strategic and purposeful. And our ability to be strategic and purposeful, is based on us collectively thinking:

Missionally*: make a positive impact in business and society*

Strategically*: help people and organizations do better*

Tactically*: develop, deliver and support great solutions*

Culturally*: inspiring, fun, team-oriented, family-centric*

Operationally*: structured, accountable, process-driven*

Financially: *do the math; be transparent; meet or exceed*

Once again, welcome aboard. Thanks for being here.

I wish you the best for a super career, and a great life.

Sincerely.

Your CEO, Level-UP, Corp.

PS: Please enjoy the enclosed book, Level-UP. *It rocks!*

Now, while the letter is a pretty decent introduction to the overall expectations of the company, and generic enough that it can apply to most any types of organizations, it certainly doesn't do complete justice to the underlying principles, realities and requirements with respect to many of the areas and expectations that the CEO wrote about.

So let's dig a little deeper.

For starters, are you prepared and ready for the #1 truth of business? By this, I mean the raw, unadulterated, butt-naked, matter-of-fact, in-your-face, clear-cut, unemotional, don't-hold-back, give-it-to-me-straight, tell-it-like-it-is, eyes-wide-open, with Jack Nicholson from the movie *A Few Good Men* shouting "you-can't-handle-the-truth" kind of truth?

Here it is:

Companies are in business to generate profitable revenues
(operative word/goal being <u>profits</u>)

Don't get this wrong: profitable revenues at the expense of corporate responsibility are inexcusable. My apologies (not) to the Gordon Geckos of the world (he's the rascally sleaze from the movie *Wall Street*, whose famous/infamous line was, "greed is good")… but greed is not good.

Corrupt, monetary greed is what gives the word "corporate" a bum rap.

You see, **companies** in-and-of themselves aren't corrupt: **people** are.

Companies don't lie, cheat, and cook the books: **people** do.

Companies don't mess-up the environment: **people** do.

Companies don't fail people: **people** fail companies.

Companies don't succeed: **people** drive a company's success.

Companies are nothing, or they're something: because of **PEOPLE**.

Even a great strategy or phenomenal products (and buckets of cash), can't make it happen without **people**. Because the fact is, a company's most important assets, and conversely, its biggest liabilities, are **people**.

People are Good.
(if they're good and talented)

Net/net: In business, the bottom line is <u>the bottom line</u>.

But let's assume that you don't fully understand the "bottom-line" expression, and that you only have a smattering of knowledge about corporate finance. No worries, because I'm going to give you a brief overview of some essential economics that everyone should know.

By the way, I never took any classes in economics or finance. In college, I was a Communications major, with a minor in English. (Yeah, you couldn't tell by the writing, could you?) In hindsight, that was a big problem with my Liberal Arts focus, and I hope that in most colleges today, those shortcomings have been corrected. You tell me.

More truth be told, although I've spent my entire career in technology, I never actually took any classes in that, either. It's pitiful to think that I graduated from college assuming P&L was something like a BLT; that a byte was something bigger than a nibble, and that EBITDA (which is an acronym that stands for "Earnings Before Interest, Tax, Depreciation and Amortization,"), could have been that pop band from Sweden.

Come to think of it, that pop band was ABBA. Mama Mia!

————————————

Let's talk numbers, because we like them. We like them a lot.

Everything in business needs to be explained, measured and justified through math (and not just simple math). If we can't do the rigorous financial analysis and show proof-positive (or close to) results using real numbers that can (relatively) prove real revenues and profits... then we don't do the business, unless we're willing to take risks. At the very least, we have to modify our thinking and expectations. If we can't do the math to rationalize new investments, new products, new strategies, new employees or new equipment, then we don't.

We save our money.

Unexplainable Spending is Bad.

Saving Money is Good.

Companies cannot be started or managed on theory, speculation and guesstimates. They can't be built on just good intentions, well-written strategy, or eloquent business plans. Don't care if you're a tiny, home-based business or a small, midsized or *Fortune 1000* corporation... you've got to do the real (and excruciating) math — details and all.

At the same time, we need to be careful — as numbers don't always tell the whole story. While numbers shouldn't lie in-and-of themselves, they're not always accurate, and don't always tell the facts. It's been said that 62 percent of all stats are worthless, and 20 percent suspect.

Enough rambling already, let's get cooking.

Come to think of it, that's not a good expression to use when talking finance, as "cooking the books" is bad. Speaking of the books, most companies use what are referred to as financial statements (the books) to establish, measure and prove the overall health of the company.

There are three standard financial statements that are GAAP compliant. GAAP stands for Generally Accepted Accounting Principles. You might hear that acronym, so it helps to know what it means. GAAP means that the business is following an approved, standardized format and formula for measuring, managing and reporting the financials.

Standards are Good.

First, there's the income statement, which describes how much was sold, the costs of what was sold, and how much profit was made, or how much money was lost. This is also more widely known as the P&L, which, as you have already learned if you didn't skip ahead, stands for the profit and loss statement. It really is the standard for measuring how profitable or not a business was (or will be) over a period of time, typically monthly, quarterly and annually. Keep in mind that within a company, there can also be numerous P&Ls as each product line, service or division can have their own, according to how the business separates and/or combines itself. For example, there can be one P&L that includes everything in a kid's combo meal, i.e. the burger, fries, drink and toy, and treats it as one item using one P&L. Likewise, there can also be separate P&Ls for measuring the individual hamburgers, fries, drinks and sundries (man, I'm getting hungry again).

The four basic elements of the P&L are:

Gross Sales

(represents sales from all sources)

Gross Profit

(deducts costs from gross sales)

Expenses

(operating, selling, and administrative)

Net Profit

(subtracts expenses from gross profit)

Some businesspeople like to read the P&L from top to bottom. In other words, revenue first, then cost, then profit. Other people, including myself, prefer to read it from bottom to top… as profits and the cash it generates always matters more than revenues.

In their entirety, the P&L represents the business's overall sales, expenses and earnings over a period of time. While it's used as a separate, standalone tool to help manage, measure, drive, anticipate and adjust specific business within the company, it also ties into the company's <u>general ledger</u>. The general ledger ties together the financial records, which in turn, is used for the <u>balance sheet</u>.

The balance sheet is a "snapshot" of the company's overall financial standing at the present time, or in a specific moment in and of time. It documents and profiles what the company owns (which are its **assets**) and what it owes (which are its **liabilities**). At the beginning, middle and end of the day, the balance sheet should always balance with regard to assets equaling their liabilities' worth. Make sense?

The three basic elements of the balance sheet are:

- **Assets:** what the business owns plus its net worth, including assets that can be liquidated like cash, accounts receivables and inventory, long-term or fixed assets like equipment and real estate and other assets like patents and intellectual property.

- **Liabilities:** what the business owes.

- **Equity or Net Worth:** often called the "book value" of the company, it's basically the difference between assets and liabilities. In addition to book value, we also have what's called "goodwill," which includes the other assets of a company, like its brand, reputation and market share. Goodwill is used to determine additional value and price for the company.

The third financial statement is more important to home-based, small and midsize companies, most of which don't have the same size bank account and credit as the big guys. It's called the <u>cash flow</u> statement.

For all intents and purposes, the cash flow statement is the best and most appropriate measurement of a company's day-to-day ability to pay their bills, make payroll, and basically stay open for business.

Cash flow statements also help in:

- Anticipating problems

- Uncovering obstacles and issues

- Deliberating about investments

- Determining a change in direction

- Other business activities that depend on the companies' ability to take in cash, manage cash or spend (and save) cash

Cash flow, and credit to a lesser degree, is a company's lifeline — just like it is with your own personal bank account and credit cards.

Imagine that after an expensive, fun-filled weekend, you find yourself with only fifty bucks in your checking account on Monday and you don't get paid until Friday. Has that ever happened to you? Well, it's going to be hard to pay the cash-required bills that are due that week, let alone feed yourself or go out for a night on the town — unless you're willing and ready to bounce some checks, use a high-interest credit card (if you can) or one of those rip-off cash-forwarding services. Clearly, that's not the way to do it.

So mind your cash flow and credit.

Credit is nice (if you can pay it off).

But cash is king, in business and in life.

This also goes to prove the point that for most companies, profitable revenues, the cash that it generates and the credit that it can establish, are the most important financial aspects in terms of being successful.

Here's the deal: while revenues are nice, they don't pay the bills (not really). Profits are what really pay the bills, especially over time. If you make enough profits and can save them, that also helps pay the bills in the future (there's always bills). Or you can reinvest some back into the business, for growth and expansion. Or give raises, cash dividends and bonuses. That's why we like profits and cash most of all. Better yet, after-tax net profits, i.e. the cash that you get to keep (versus that EBITDA stuff), because that's the truest justification for getting paid, getting raises, dividends, bonuses and the overall value of the business.

Cash is Good.

This also validates another major point, in that good and accurate information and communication is invaluable — not just information that pertains to the numbers and the economics, but to everything.

When conducting business, especially when we are in meetings, or sending e-mails and other types of written correspondence, we typically don't have a lot of time for a lot of words, wavering thoughts, rambling sentences, and idle chatter. (Yeah, I know what you're thinking — something about that being ironic coming from me. But hey, this is my book after all, so it gives me permission to be more "talkative.")

In most businesses, we like to keep things focused: short and simple, but not simplistic. We say what we mean, and mean what we say.

With precision and timeliness.

When writing or talking to someone on a business level and discussing business objectives, we should always keep in the front of our mind two words whenever contemplating content, direction, scope and overall purpose of our communication. Those two words are:

"So What?"

Before we write what we write, and say what we say, we need to ask ourselves, "What am I trying to do? What am I trying to accomplish? What's my goal? What's the expected or desired outcome, action or result of my communication?" In other words, if we can't answer the "so-what" question — then keep working on it, or just forget about it.

Depending on the situation, sometimes less is more.

Sometimes more is more.

And sometimes it's best to stay quiet.

When in doubt — stay quiet.

To sum it up, good companies need viable and valued products, and/or services, and/or solutions. They also need good operations, systems, infrastructure and the technology to help market, sell, fulfill, measure, stay informed and support their products, services and solutions. Most importantly, they need good and talented people to get everything done.

And remember, although revenue's important, as that's ultimately how we get to profits, profits matter more — especially after-tax profits, the cash it generates and how it's used to enhance the company's value, grow the business, make payroll, give raises, and bonuses.

Bonuses are Good.

And always appreciated.

Always.

Know Your Company
(and the company you keep)

According to the author William Ward, who's truly got some fantastic quotes, there are four steps to achievement:

- To plan purposefully

- Prepare prayerfully

- Proceed positively

- Pursue persistently

I think these steps correlate well with how you should start your new job, whether you're already onboard, or just getting ready. You see, the better you know your company and your specific *to-dos*, the better you'll perform. The better you perform, the more you can help your colleagues, and the more quickly you can contribute and excel.

Performing is Good.

Speaking of jobs, they're not always easy to get, especially those that you might want and have schooling or even training and experience in. You might have to take a job you don't want, just to get your foot in the door or most importantly, to earn paychecks.

As it pertains to work, sometimes we have to do what we have to do.

I think it's neat how Martin Luther King put it,

> *"If a man is called to be a street sweeper, he should sweep streets even as Michelangelo painted, or Beethoven composed music, or Shakespeare wrote poetry. He should sweep streets so well that all the hosts of heaven and Earth will pause to say, 'Here lived a great street sweeper who did his job well.'"*

I'd also add that just because we start as a street sweeper, doesn't mean that we'll always be one — especially if our PAAM and work ethic are as Dr. King suggested. There are countless examples of this, where young people have not only accepted jobs that they didn't really want, but did them with passion, energy and desire. More importantly, they performed exceptionally well, delivering quick results.

Heck, if I can do it, so can you.

You see, after graduating from college, the best job I could get was as a telemarketer, making about eighty calls a day. That wasn't the dream. Fast forward a few months later, dejected and downtrodden, I saw an infomercial after the David Letterman show from motivator, Tony Robbins. I bought the tapes, which set me back a couple hundred bucks that I couldn't afford. You know what, though? It worked. I listened to what he had to say, applying not just his techniques, but more importantly his spirit for life — his PAAM. Within months of finishing the program, and after making a renewed commitment to myself and the job, I produced big sales in short-order. As a result, I was promoted and transferred to lead outside sales in a new branch office. Score!

Please understand that I'm not telling you that to be a show-off or to "toot my own horn," although sometimes in life you have to humbly toot your own horn, especially if others won't toot it for you. This strategy is best used when interviewing for a job, seeking a promotion or asking for a raise. This is incorrectly used on your first date, or if you can't live up to the music, and you get busted for wrongful tooting.

Wrongful Tooting is Bad.

I know from personal experience and from witnessing others, that if we have the right PAAM, we can overcome most any obstacle.

Granted, it takes plenty of work, stick-to-itiveness and perseverance.

No one said it would be easy.

President Calvin Coolidge said,

> *"Nothing in the world can take the place of perseverance.*
> *Talent will not; nothing is more common than unsuccessful*
> *individuals with talent. Genius will not; unrewarded genius is almost*
> *a proverb. Education will not; the world is full of educated derelicts.*
> *Persistence and determination alone are omnipotent."*

Persistence & Determination are Good.

So again, as far as your new job goes, you need to take the time to study the company and anything that pertains to the company, as it's very impressive to see a well-prepared interviewee or new employee. As you know already, you never get a second chance to make a good first impression; so make it a good one. Better yet, make it a series of good ones... as you will certainly be meeting, seeing and working with lots of new people. These people, in turn, may talk about you to other people, and in turn, other people. And so on, and so on.

People talk.

This brings me to the second use of the word "company," and that's the company you keep within the company. Specifically, it's the people you befriend and associate with inside and outside of work. Which brings me back to the aforementioned "creeping-meatball" theory.

Company meatballs — and no, I'm not talking about what we put into spaghetti, stuff in a bun, or eat from a stick — are the types of people who act like those meatballs. You know, sitting around, soaking up the sauce, and basically doing nothing. Meatballs are slackers, folks with bad attitudes who do less than their fair share, but bitch and moan about the workload, nevertheless. Meatballs talk too much and work too little. They tend to badmouth the performers that get things done. More often than not, meatballs like to bellyache about the company's issues (all companies have issues), whether they're real or imaginary. Company meatballs are bad, as opposed to barbecued meatballs, which are good.

Here are some differences between performers and meatballs:

- **Performers** work hard, work smart and get things done.

  Meatballs just go through the motions.

- **Performers** are players who score.

  Meatballs are spectators who just keep the score.

- **Performers** win, lose and take calculated risks.

  Meatballs do neither.

- **Performers** talk about "we" and "us" and "our."

  Meatballs talk about "they" and "them."

- **Performers** get it done and make it happen.

  Meatballs get in the way and watch it happen.

- **Performers** do it in real time, all the time.

  Meatballs need replays and do-overs.

- **Performers** have pride and are paid to perform.

  Meatballs just want to get paid.

Net/Net:

Performers execute.

Meatballs don't.

(By the way, you'll find out that the words <u>execute</u> and <u>execution</u> are two of the most important, and more often than not, most overused but underperformed words in business. To read a great book on execution, check out *Six Disciplines Execution Revolution* by Gary Harpst.)

To compound the problem, meatballs are also always looking to recruit others to be in their meatball gang, especially young and vulnerable new employees who may not know any better. If you're not careful, you'll find yourself directly or indirectly associated with them.

Worst of all, you could find yourself joining them.

That's how we get *creeping meatballism.*

So be careful of the meatballs.

The best defense against this is a good offense. A good offense means being a performer who performs and is known for performing. So be a performer, or for reasons I'll never understand, be a meatball. But please, on behalf of everyone, don't ever be a meatball disguised as a performer. That's just wrong.

And you want to know what's even worse than creeping meatballs?

Zombie creeping meatballs.

That's real trouble.

Alright already: enough about meatballs. For one, it's making me hungry. Two, it doesn't deserve any more time. What does deserve more time and appreciation is one of the most important elements in business (and life, for that matter), and it's summed up in one word:

EXPECTATIONS

One of the best things that we can do to ensure short-term and long-term satisfaction, achievable results and success (as opposed to frustration and failure), is to set realistic and achievable expectations.

While we appreciate the fact that (talented) people are critical and make the ultimate difference, and that companies need good products and good customer service, as well as the operations, systems, and technology infrastructure to market, sell and support themselves — we can't get where we want to go comfortably, without setting realistic expectations. And these expectations need to be rationalized and supported by good reasoning and explainable economics.

Nike's "**Just Do It**" mentality is cool for working out, but that maxim will get us into trouble in business. Everything we do should be planned and have understandable expectations, especially what we control. Unfortunately, while most of us would agree that expectations need to be real and realistic, you'll find that lots businesspeople (and lots of older adults, for that matter), don't share that same view.

Due to the constant pressures that every company has to sell more, save more, do more, and make more... some people inappropriately set unrealistic expectations. They might sound bold and adventurous on the front-end, but they'll get them into potential trouble on the back-end, when they're unable to meet, let alone exceed, those expectations.

I'd also like to make a distinction between **expectations** and **goals**. There is a difference, as goals should be subordinate to expectations. For example, it's all right to set "stretch-goals," which in theory are typically goals that go above and beyond the primary expectation. If you hit the stretch-goals, great! If you don't, you at least should have met the original expectation. You'll hear a lot about stretch-goals in business. Likewise, you'll hear a lot about exceeding expectations.

While all of us should be fans of exceeding expectations (as long as they're based on reality), we need to watch out if our job is set-up for constantly making its stretch-goals and exceeding expectations. If that's an expectation, it's a bad one. Try to avoid that. If you always work from and are measured on bad expectations, it's going to be difficult and painful. Over time, it's going to cause frustration.

Frustration is Bad.

Let's bring back the CEO of Level-UP, Corp. so that she can frame her expectations. This should give you a feel for what a company might expect from a high-level, broad-strokes goals/expectations standpoint:

Each of us sets demanding, yet realistic expectations — as well as a comprehensive portfolio of goals that, when achieved, make the person, our organization, and our company, winners. In addition, we expect each and every one of us to say what we mean, and do what we say.

We will meet or exceed realistic expectations with courtesy, respect and appreciation. It is our responsibility to communicate what's going on with simplicity and clarity. We will be known for doing what we say we'll do, on time, with smiles and good cheer. We'll work fast, but we won't hurry. When we hurry, mistakes happen (haste makes waste). Our clients will like us for what we do, how we do it, and who we are. We work for our clients. We're a team. We also know that continuous improvement is critical. Everything in our business, including us personally, can be improved and should get better, every day. In other words – we can always be "leveling-up," as the expression goes.

In summary:

- *We expect everyone to understand our priorities*

- *We expect to meet or exceed individual goals and objectives*

- *We expect uncompromising teamwork, empathy, and support*

- *We expect excellence and a commitment to accountability*

- *We expect everyone to do their jobs, and do their best at them*

- *We expect leadership, innovation, trust, kindness, and fun*

- *We expect to achieve growth and exceptional client service*

- *We expect everyone to say what they mean, and do what they say*

- *We expect to celebrate the good; and resolve the bad*

- *We expect to develop/deliver/support high-quality solutions*

- *We expect to work fast, but not to hurry*

- *We expect to produce profitable revenues*

There you have it: our CEO's goals and expectations framework. It stands to reason that the leaders of your company will (hopefully) share many of the same views, goals and expectations as her. If you can understand and live up to most of those, you're good to go. Cool?

Let's close this section on another important topic:

LEADERSHIP

Good Leadership is Good.

Notice the use of the word *good* versus more dynamic adverbs like *awesome, remarkable, extraordinary, fantastic, brilliant* or *incredible*. Undoubtedly, you've already noticed the extensive usage of the word *good* (and *bad*) throughout the book already. The reason is simple; while there may be lots of big adjectives that have more impact and panache than *good* — good is still good (and *bad* is still bad).

WHEN IT COMES TO GOOD LEADERSHIP, GOOD IS GREAT

Sadly, good leadership is in short supply; which is a big problem for business. As such, it's impacting our society, economy and the country in general. You see, good leaders aren't just the folks who run and manage organizations. Good leaders can also be the folks who sweep the floors. Good leaders aren't always the smartest or best performers. Leaders and leadership is not something that's anointed or bought, given because of someone's title or their place in a hierarchical organization chart. Good leaders and good leadership are earned. It's not entitled or bequeathed. That said, we all need to do a better job at trying to be good leaders, and to a degree, do a better job of being good **followers** — with a willingness to do all of the jobs. All of the time.

If you want a startling insight into the magnitude of this "do the job" problem... specifically that as a nation we might be falling behind some other countries like India and China with regard to our work ethic and work mentality... you're encouraged to read an extremely compelling book by Thomas Friedman called, *The World is Flat.*

It's an astonishing, eye-opening commentary for our country with regard to our individual and collective attitude and responsibilities about labor, as well as the importance of us being good leaders. It also tells us we need to be diligent workers; willing and able to do what it takes to keep the jobs. If we're not careful and if we don't figure out how to better manage and compete with what's happening in regard to globalization and offshoring, we could be in a really sticky situation.

The fact is, we're in one now (it's pretty much a perpetual thing).

As you may know, offshoring is when companies send work to foreign countries, for cheaper labor. And not just manufacturing jobs and programming, but professions like engineering, management, research and development, accounting, drug discovery, legal, web design, etc.

At the risk of sounding like an alarmist, if we're not vigilant, we could find ourselves in an even bigger predicament, especially if we don't accept this reality, deal with it, and co-exist. Personally, I'm a fan of "right-shoring" — which is a middle-of-the-road, best-of-both strategy.

Excuse my tangent here, but couple this excessive and often overdone offshoring movement... with our expensive, messed-up healthcare system... then throw in the certainty of global warming (if you haven't seen the movie *An Inconvenient Truth*, please do so, but without letting politics get in the way)... and we now have some potential trouble brewing — for us, our economy, society, and the industry of America.

Indeed, in the laws of trickle-down economics, we could see real problems for our country, and subsequently, present generations and those generations after us. If you haven't read Friedman's book, please read it. If you haven't seen the movie, or read-up on the issues with regard to our environment (that includes both sides), please do so.

If you don't do either, consider yourself forewarned.

Forewarned is Good.

Indifference is Bad.

I have a colleague and friend who is dealing firsthand with this offshoring reality in the heartland of America. He's running a project with a Japanese company that has a manufacturing plant in northern Kentucky. They recently bought some new enterprise-resource-planning software, or ERP, and needed to install it quickly and cheaply. (In case you want to know, ERP is the catch-all name for the software that many companies use to help to run, manage, measure and report. It can be very complex and cumbersome. It can also be extremely costly, as the software itself is typically not cheap, and the work it takes to implement is more often than not, even more expensive. Hairy stuff.)

Anyhow, in order to keep costs low, some companies are having to offshore this work to foreign firms in foreign countries because many of the U.S.-based outfits are too expensive. In this case however, the other shore came to the States. Due to the type of work required, they've flown in four very talented, experienced, college-educated programmers from another country, who collectively live in a two-bedroom hotel; cook on hot plates, and eat from paper plates.

They work fourteen-hour days and make minimum wage in accordance to U.S. standards. They're busting their butts and making next to nothing. But if you asked them, however, they would tell you that it's great; that they're having fun, learning lots and digging America. They'd also tell you that they're thankful for their jobs, but most of all, that they're making money, even though they miss their families and are living in those conditions for an indefinite period of time.

Are you willing to do that?

Are you willing to fly thirty hours every few weeks, live in a crummy hotel, work fourteen-hour days, and miss your family and friends and all your stuff for pay you think is inferior to your standards? Are you?

Tangent over. Let's get back to talking about leadership.

So here's a truckload of the key leadership qualities, attributes and characteristics that make for a good leader. For that matter, these qualities make for good employees, good colleagues, good friends, and good people. Just remember, while it's easy to write and read about them in a book... it's a whole other thing to actually internalize them, embrace them, use them and more importantly, be them. For sure.

Learning to be a good leader is a lifelong journey, a journey that will never end (hopefully). But you have to start somewhere and do something — no matter whom you are, or where you come from. An embodiment of this resolute determination is Elihu Burritt, a poor, "learned blacksmith," born in America in 1810. He was known for his self-improvement, writing and pacifism. He became a highly regarded social reformist respected by prominent leaders around the world.

With regard to his life, Elihu wrote,

> *"All that I have accomplished has been by the plodding, patient, persevering process of accretion, which build the ant heap particle by particle, thought by thought, fact by fact."*

If a blacksmith in the 1800s... without the tools and support you have today... can become a renowned leader by intestinal fortitude, gutsy perseverance, and noble determination... you can as well, can't you?

Particle by particle.

Thought by thought.

Fact by fact.

Good Leaders...

Good Leaders have integrity.
They are ethical, humble, compassionate, trustworthy.

Good Leaders are stractical.
They are good with both strategy and being tactical.

Good Leaders are realistic.
They have achievable expectations, goals and objectives.

Good Leaders execute.
They get things done on time and on budget.

Good Leaders comprehend the economics.
They do the math and know how to measure.

Good Leaders are productive.
They like productivity, efficiency, and effectiveness.

Good Leaders are good collaborators and communicators.
They're understandable, and they understand.

Good Leaders are energetic and motivated.
They work hard and have fun with it.

Good Leaders are team players.
They are empathetic, likable and others-oriented.

Good Leaders anticipate, adapt and adopt.
They're flexible.

Good Leaders are accountable.
They are organized and coordinated. They deliver.

Good Leaders think outside and inside "the box."
They get momentum and progress.

Good Leaders are knowledgeable.
They have real skills and broad perspectives.

Good Leaders have conviction and are committed.
They work hard and smart.

Good Leaders keep things simple, not simplistic.
They know the difference.

Good Leaders have a "why."
They know it's about more than just making money.

Good Leaders are authentic.
They have humble confidence and positive pragmatism.

Good Leaders do the hard and soft stuff.
They can manage the books and the feelings.

Good Leaders listen intently.
They hear what people say and what they mean.

Good Leaders rally for good change.
They justify, promote, manage and deliver change.

Good Leaders are comfortable with ambiguity and uncertainty.
They also like details.

Good Leaders handle the pressure.
They're thick-skinned and cool under duress.

Good Leaders have solid memories.
They remember and forget appropriately.

Good Leaders are self-critical.
They know that they make mistakes and can improve.

Good Leaders know when enough is enough.
They put first things first.

Good Leaders are coaches.
They want and nurture more good leaders.

Good Leaders appreciate a balanced life.
They get it; live it; give it.

Good Leaders are also diplomatic, persistent and persevering, agreeable, unassuming, calm, polite, good-humored, exciting and excited, helpful, thoughtful, competitive, steady, brave, self-starting, conscientious, earnest, flexible, resolute, tolerant, spirited, cheerful, inclusive, congenial, patient, responsive, trusting, optimistic, loyal, and consistent. (Note: nothing frustrates employees more than convenient, inconsistent, disingenuous, in-title-only leaders; blaaaaaaaaaahhhhh.)

Now, I know you're thinking, *"Gee, Scott, that's a lot."*

Indeed it is.

It just goes to show you that it's not easy, or probably even possible for that matter, to have all of those qualities and characteristics. Not really.

But here's the great news: you don't have to.

For what it's worth, nobody has all those attributes.

Nobody.

Even if they have most of them, they always need work and can always improve, and they'll be the first to admit it. At least the best ones will.

Take it one day at a time. Be mindful of what makes a good leader, and start to work at it: particle by particle, thought by thought, fact by fact.

If you do want to learn more about business leadership, you should at least read two books — *The Leadership Challenge* by Kouzes and Posner, and *True North* by Bill George with Peter Sims. Good stuff.

———————

There's an old parable about a guy walking down the street, who happens to see a bricklayer laying bricks (after all, that's what they do, right). Curious as to what was being built, the man walked up and asked the bricklayer what he was doing? The brick layer gruffly replied, "What's it look like I'm doing? I'm laying bricks." At that, the man walked around the corner, and saw another bricklayer who was laying bricks, as well. He decided to ask this man the same question. But this worker, however, proudly replied, "I'm building a cathedral."

So, are you building a cathedral?

Or just laying bricks?

To help sum up and simplify the core elements of any good business, just remember my supercalifragilisticexpialidocious **P5 Formula**.

PEOPLE

People are the most important asset of any organization, regardless of its size, industry or location. Whether it's public or private, for profit or not-for-profit, or even highly automated, and technology driven... it makes no difference when it comes to the importance of people. Especially good and talented people, who are team-oriented, hard-working, reliable, nice and have proper values and the right PAAM.

(Good) People are Good.

PRODUCTS

It certainly helps to have good products (which can also be services and/or solutions) that people and other companies need, and want, to buy. And hopefully, buy a lot of it. Keep in mind that companies and people buy stuff because they think it has value, and that it can and will do something for them in such a way that it motivates them to purchase it at a price that they can rationalize, from both a quantitative standpoint (i.e. price, affordability, ROI, etc.) and from a qualitative standpoint, in that it makes them feel better emotionally, physically, spiritually, etc..

(Good) Products are Good.

PROCESS

This is also referred to, and falls under the heading of operations, logistics, and supply-chain management (remember ERP?). Process and procedure is how/what a business does tactically and systematically to perform, manage and measure. In effect, this is how it executes and gets things done. Companies need to be as efficient, effective and productive as they can be — so the differences between good processes and bad processes can be incredibly significant — impacting not only customer service, sales and profits but teamwork, attitude and morale.

(Good) Process is Good.

PLANNING

This is where we do the work with regard to vision and strategy, but also with regard to improving the here-and-now. Companies, like people, must always be planning for change and progress. That includes planning for how to enhance the present and deal with the future in regard to competition, unforeseen problems, disruptions from new technology and products, employee attrition, changes in socio-economic policy, you name it. No business can exist long-term if they don't properly plan, change, measure, anticipate and improve.

(Good) Planning is Good.

PROFITS

Businesses are in business to generate profitable revenues, so they can pay for their people, products, processes, and planning; in other words, so they can exist. Only by existing, can they provide jobs with paychecks. Be responsible. Generate value. Pay taxes. Donate to charities that help the community that the business and employees live in. Build new products, services, or solutions. Hire more people. Give raises, dividends and bonuses. And grow. While many businesses start without profit and/or use debt, that's only acceptable if the expectation is to repay those debts. You can only do that through the cash that comes from profit. Revenues are good. Profits are great. Cash is king.

(Good) Profits are Good.

And that my friend, is the

P5 Formula

Learn it.

Know it.

Embrace it.

PUTTING IT ALL TOGETHER, AND GETTING IT ALL DONE

You're the Architect, Builder and Custodian of Your Own Success

"We may affirm absolutely that nothing great in the world has been accomplished without passion."

GEORG HEGEL

In the spirit of sharing and caring, allow me to express some final recommendations, with the sincere hope that these closing comments, along with the other ideas and suggestions — will help you be a better **architect**, **builder** and **custodian** of your own success and happiness.

Assuming that happens, I ask that you "pay it forward."

When you're ready, and certain that the time is right, take the initiative and be a good mentor yourself. You don't have to write a book; just be a good coach, or at a minimum, a supportive friend. When you're ready, offer guidance and support to someone who can use your help.

Help is Good.
Being Helpful Even Better.

Speaking of being helpful... I keep two Father's Day cards at my desk: one from my parents, and one from my wife. On the cover of the card from my parents is a picture of a young boy dressed in goggles, wearing one of those old-fashioned pilot's caps with the flaps that hang down over the ears. He's standing on a box, with a towel wrapped around him like a cape. His arms are stretched out wide as if he is flying. He has a big smile and a marvelous look of pure enjoyment. The writing with the picture says, *"Son, from playing the hero..."* Then when you open the card, there's another picture of a grown man, walking on the beach with his child sitting on his shoulders, holding onto Dad's hands. They're playing happily in the waves. The caption underneath this picture, and in an obvious continuation of the sentiment from the cover reads, *"...To being the hero."* Then on the other side of the card is written: *"How wonderful it has been to watch you grow into the amazing man you are. Happy Father's Day."* Then it's signed simply, *"Love You, Mom and Dad."*

Now inside the card from my wife is a picture of our two children, happy as all get-out. Opposite of the picture are the following words: *"'Walk a little slower, Daddy,' said a child so small. 'I'm following in your footsteps, and I don't want to fall. Sometimes your steps are very fast. Sometimes they're hard to see; so walk a little slower, Daddy, for you are leading me. Someday when I'm all grown up, you're what I want to be. Then I will have a little child who'll want to follow me. And I would want to lead just right, and know that I was true. So walk a little slower, Daddy, for I must follow you.'"*

I have to tell you, about a week or so after getting those cards, I brought them into my office and read them again, maybe ten times or more. They made me cry — and I'm not just talking about getting watery eyed. That happens even when I watch sappy TV. I'm talking about a caught-off-guard, grimacing, tears-rolling-down-my-face-cry.

Talk about a Hallmark moment.

In hindsight, I don't really know why the cards affected me like they did. Maybe I was having a bad day, or had been short-tempered with my kids earlier that morning, and it made me remorseful. Or maybe it was because I really didn't think that I was worth such neat cards.

Regardless, they did something besides generate tears.

They still do.

The cards make me stop and reflect. They motivate me, and make me appreciative of all that life has to offer, as well as the responsibilities and obligations that we have in life. The cards also impress upon me the fact that we have to be mindful of everything, that everything matters and even what doesn't matter, matters.

You see, if it matters to you, but not to somebody else, it certainly matters, right? Intuitively then, if it matters to somebody else, but not to you, it still matters though, because it matters to that person.

That's why the so-called "**Golden Rule**" is somewhat flawed — from both a sentiment and a wordsmithing standpoint. Frankly, it shouldn't be, "Treat people the way *you* want to be treated." After all, "you" could be a real jerk, and think it's okay to treat, and be treated, like a jerk. What the "Golden Rule" actually should say is, "Treat people the way *they* want to be treated." That's assuming they're not some devil-worshipping, psycho sadomasochist into bad music. That is not good.

But seriously, it's not just a difference in wordsmithing — it's not.

There's a fundamental differentiation in the philosophy between the two interpretations. Simply stated, one's *self-oriented* and one's *others-oriented*. Because you're savvy, you'll agree. As importantly, you'll appreciate the difference and choose the right one.

After all, you're big enough to read this book, willing enough to get this far, and smart enough to hang in there until the very end (you're still here, right?). That says something about your ability to learn, to be challenged and to accept different interpretations and points of view.

That said, there will be those who disagree with us (assuming we think alike) and pundits who will say that we're overly sensitive, and just not tough enough. That's okay. They can, and should, have their own opinions. After all, opinions are like belly buttons — we all have them.

How you manage them, however, is the real trick.

The writer F. Scott Fitzgerald said,

> *"The ability to hold two opposing ideas in mind at the same time and still retain the ability to function, is the sign of a truly intelligent person."*

And you can do that, can't you?

Again and as always, everything matters.

Even what doesn't.

Most of all...

IT MATTERS that you respect the fact that you, and you alone, are the **architect, builder** and **custodian** of your life. You're in charge.

IT MATTERS that we're compassionate. There's a terrific book by Harry Palmer called *Resurfacing: Techniques for Exploring Consciousness* that recommends a five-step-exercise for putting compassion in action. It goes like this: With your attention focused on the other person, be it a friend or stranger, tell yourself that:

1: "Just like me, this person is seeking happiness."

2: "Just like me, this person is trying to avoid suffering."

3: "Just like me, this person knows sadness and despair."

4: "Just like me, this person is seeking to fill needs."

5: "Just like me, this person is learning about life."

IT MATTERS that we go to work and that we do our best work. But it also matters that we do so smartly, and in recognition of why we work, which is to provide for and secure that which is important.

IT MATTERS that there is too much violence, hatred, injustice, pain and suffering. We need to do what we can, in our own way, to help the discriminated against, the sick, the under-resourced and less fortunate.

IT MATTERS that we have values and ethics, that we can be trusted and trust, that we listen and learn, and that we're others-oriented.

IT MATTERS that we can be individuals with individuality, but that we can also be sensitive, others-oriented and mindful of what others think, feel and what they're going through.

IT MATTERS that we are disciplined and personally accountable; that we do what we say and say what we'll do, and that we can take and accept criticism and respond accordingly.

IT MATTERS that we can promote, embrace, manage and deliver change; that we are both realistic and idealistic, and that we know the difference between when, where and why. Think positive pragmatism.

IT MATTERS that we can disagree agreeably... and that we can take the high-road, move-on, and turn the proverbial other cheek.

IT MATTERS that we keep tabs on our finances, and manage our cash flow and credit; that we only spend what we can, and only buy what we should. Debt stinks (especially when it's expensive, high interest debt).

IT MATTERS that we care for our environment and deal with the "inconvenient truth" of pollution and global warming; that we respect our world and do our part to keep it clean and healthy.

IT MATTERS that we're always improving ourselves: minds, bodies, values and spirit. It matters that we promote quality in work, and life.

IT MATTERS that we love unconditionally, and that we bestow love and receive love unconditionally (as best we can, of course). It also matters that we parent conditionally, and respect the job of parenting.

IT MATTERS that we appreciate our individual and collective responsibilities to ourselves, our families and our friends — and yes, our companies, colleagues, country and world. Be fully accountable.

IT MATTERS that we laugh, listen to music, sing, dance, stay fit, read, work, enjoy life, learn and strive to be genuinely exceptional.

(Take some time to think about your own unique "**IT MATTERS**." Talk about it with family and friends. Think big and important.)

On that note, let's end the book just as it started: by thanking you.

Thanks for your time, mind, heart, body and spirit.

While I can't express my gratitude in person and give you a friendly hug, I want you to know that your commitment to being the very best that you can be, and having the right PAAM will mean a lot to the company you work for, as well as the company you keep.

Your success is significant to your friends, our country and whether you can see it or believe it, our planet. Most importantly of all, your success means so very much on the behalf of family, yours and others'. That includes grandparents and parents, as well as yours and other people's children.

So while good first impressions are important, remember to make good lasting impressions that mean something now, and after we're gone.

What should people say about you today?

What do you want them to say about you today?

And how do you want to be known, tomorrow and beyond?

Swami Sivananda said, *"Put your heart, mind, intellect and soul even into your smallest acts. This is the secret to success."* And to quote William Ward again, *"Do more than belong; participate. Do more than care; help. Do more than believe; practice. Do more than be fair; be kind. Do more than forgive; forget. Do more than dream; work."*

And that my friend, is what it's all about.

What you put into you...

How you manage and develop you...

To help make you and us the best professionals that we can be.

So that we can accelerate our mutual success…

Enjoy good careers and good livelihoods…

And live full, loving, compassionate, family-oriented…

Time of our life lives.

That's All Good.

And remember (always) Level-UP.

Now and forever.

Leveling-UP is Good.

Thanks again.

Peace and happiness to you and the world.

Peace and Happiness are Good.

AFTERWORD

*Questions for Individual
and Group Discussions*

*"Tell me and I forget; teach me and I
may remember; involve me and I learn."*

BENJAMIN FRANKLIN

In the introduction, Scott talks about his "purpose and gratitude." If you were to write a book at this time in your life, what would be your "purpose" for doing so? What would be the title? Try to incorporate a personal and professional perspective. Also, if you were to write down your gratitude to those that helped get you here, who would you thank, and why? After you have those answers, finish by writing your own "book dedication." Be sure to make it meaningful and memorable. Maybe even pass it on as a gift, to those that would appreciate that gift.

In the first chapter, there's a great deal of emphasis placed on self-awareness, and personal accountability. Why is this is so important, and do you agree? What about the sentiment that you can't effectively be "others-oriented," if you're not first and foremost self-oriented? Does that seem selfish? What does it mean to you, to be self-aware? Are you comfortable looking at yourself "objectively." Write two or three paragraphs on who *you* think you are: title that section, ME. Then, write another two or three paragraphs on how you think *others* perceive you to be: title that, OTHERS. When finished, really think about how they match up and moreover, if you want to do anything about either.

Scott believes that dealing with *change,* is both a challenge and an opportunity. He says change is one of the biggest issues we have to face at work, and life. What do you think? Is change such a big deal? If so, why? If not, why not?" (And don't cop-out and say "it depends," that answer is not allowed.) Either way, grade yourself on a scale of 1-10, on how comfortable you are with change — both the good and bad change. Assuming you think change is a good thing, what would you change about yourself today? Why? Again, think about how this change will apply to you on both a personal and a professional level.

You read about the acronym PAAM. What does it stand for, and why's it important? What do you think about your own PAAM? Is it good?

There are a lot of perceptions about the Millennial Generation. Do you agree with the whole, "perception is reality (PIR)" thing – irrespective of the Millennial part? In general, is PIR fair? Why does it happen? Next, write down specific examples of what you think are the most common perceptions about Millennials, specifically. Give some real examples of how PIR plays out in your world (as an individual), and what you can do to overcome it and/or leverage it (as an individual).

One of the book's big points is that "leveling-up" is not just about one specific act or action, but a never-ending process of self-improvement. While there are "check-the-box" types of level-up events, milestones, accomplishments, etc., he really drives home the importance of always striving to grow personally and professionally, and that we should never be complacent in making ourselves better. You agree? What are the upsides and the downsides of trying to always improve ourselves?

The refrain, "it's not personal, it's business," is used all too often. But Scott writes that "business is personal." Which sentiment do you agree with, and why? How do you feel (what's your PAAM) about business and corporations, in general? Give specific examples from your own experience, or things that you've seen or read, that makes you think the way you think. If and/or when you go to work for a company (or do so already), list what's most important for you to succeed at your specific job. If you were to start your own company, what would it be and why? Finally, take the time to write your own letter from you, the CEO.

Leadership is a major theme and subject in the book. Do you think leadership is that important? Explain. Scott covers a lot of attributes, qualities and character traits that make for good leaders. What are some of those that you think are most important, and list them in order? Feel free to go back in the book. One of the covenants that Scott's says makes for a good leader — is to be a good follower: talk about that.

Scott writes about the need for us to live a work/life balanced life. Do you think this is really possible to have work/life balance? That said, and answered — what can you do today, to help ensure that you can and will, live a happy and successful work/life balanced life. Write down your own personal-value-statement (PVS), and be sure to review, maintain and update this PVS, as your work/life progresses. Be Good!

The space below is left blank for your own Q&A.

Think Big. Be Bold. Have Fun.

SCOTT E. ABBOTT is an architect, builder and custodian of new business, growth and talent. However, he thinks of himself foremost as a son, husband, father, friend and humanist. It was in this spirit of servant leadership, coupled with what he calls his "heartfelt civic-duty" and an advocacy for energizing life's work - that he wrote **Level-UP to Professional**. When Scott's not actively working, reading, writing, sleeping and cooking (or pretending to do one of those) … he's enjoying life with his family, friends and colleagues. Please join Scott on Twitter @scottabbottabc and on Facebook.com/leveluptopro.